The Southern Plantations Cook

Featuring favorite recipes from the finest shooting plantations including Barton Ridge, Bostick, Cabin Bluff, Enon, Henderson Village, Mansfield, Pinewood, Pinway, Quail Country, and Wynfield Plantation.

The Southern Plantations Cook

Copyright © 1999 by *The Southern Plantations Cook*

Leslie Delaney
David McKim
Saint Simons Publishing
912/638-0309

All Rights Reserved.

No part of this book may be reproduced in any way
without permission from the publisher.

By
Leslie Delaney
David McKim

ISBN: 0-9671690-1-1

Printed in the USA by The Wimmer Companies, Memphis, TN

Table of Contents

Barton Ridge Plantation
page 5

Bostick Plantation
page 19

The Lodge at Cabin Bluff
page 31

Enon Plantation
page 43

Henderson Village
page 53

Mansfield Plantation
page 67

Pinewood Plantation
page 77

Pinway Plantation
page 87

Quail Country
page 99

Wynfield Plantation
page 109

Plantation Favorites
page 118

Index
page 127

Introduction

Working on this cookbook was very exciting for us.
We enjoyed visiting the plantations featured in this cookbook
and experiencing the history and charm of each plantation.
Each plantation is shown in its own glorious way with full color photographs and favorite recipes
so that you can bring home a taste to share with your friends and family.

Acknowledgements

The Plantation Pond Covey, oil painting on board, David Lanier, 1996.

The Plantation Pond Covey was the featured painting of the 1996 Plantation Wildlife Arts Festival,
a nationally acclaimed Wildlife Art Show and Sale held each November at the
Thomasville Cultural Center in Thomasville, Georgia.
The painting was purchased for the Center's permanent collection by the Parker Poe Charitable Trust.

Linda Pinson at Pinway Plantation for the photo in Plantations Favorites.

John Toth and his Staff at the Darkroom

Eddie and Rita McGuire

All the Plantations and their Staff

Barton Ridge Plantation

Barton Ridge takes you back to nature in total comfort. Hidden deep in the foothills of the Appalachian Mountains, the Plantation contains 5,000 acres of beautiful old hardwood forests, bubbling crystal clear springs, and quiet ponds all surrounded by plentiful sylvan valleys. The land is intensely managed year-round for wildlife and the hunts and fishing are superb.

The natural beauty of Barton Ridge Plantation is easily enjoyed on any of five marked hiking trails. Birders be sure to bring your field glasses as Barton Ridge is located on a major flyway, and you will be thrilled to spot one of their pair of majestic Bald Eagles. In spring, the lodge is surrounded by beautiful trees such as dogwoods, redbuds, and some of the largest tulip poplars to be seen anywhere. In fall, enjoy crisp clear days and brilliant foliage, relaxing later in front of one of their woodburning fireplaces.

In all, Barton Ridge Plantation is a world-class executive retreat. The natural beauty and serenity so hard to come by in today's hectic world are the everyday way of life at Barton Ridge Plantation.

Hunting

Barton Ridge Plantation offers quail hunts each year from October through February and turkey hunts from March through April. A typical day would include breakfast at 8:00 a.m. Following a satisfying breakfast, your guides will escort you to a field where you and your party will hunt until noon. After a successful hunt, you'll return to the Plantation Inn for a delicious lunch and a short rest. Then, it's back to the field around 2:00 p.m. for more fantastic quail hunting until dusk. After an enjoyable day of hunting, you return to the lodge for refreshing cocktails and an outstanding dinner at your leisure.

Barton Ridge Plantation has seven courses with early release and wild birds. Also available is a hunting preserve with liberated birds. The average walk per day is 2.5 to 3 miles. Over and under or side by side is the choice gun for quail hunting.

The plantation is intensively managed for all wildlife—from whitetail deer and wild turkey, to dove and quail. Hunters are accommodated by over 20 shooting houses and two handicap accessible automated stands. Fishermen have many ponds on the property to choose from, including one stocked with bass and another with catfish, as well as five streams. Barton Ridge can arrange guides for fly fishing and rafting nearby.

Dining

Barton Ridge Plantation is a wing-shooting lodge and specializes in early release and wild birds and turkeys. The pleasure of the hunting excursion is complimented by the elegant dining offered at the Plantation Inn. Their chefs prepare a wide array of cuisine, but specialize in New Southern American dishes. The Plantation Inn houses eight luxury bedrooms, along with a swimming pool, exercise room, and tennis courts. Or, you may prefer to stay in one of their fully appointed rustic cabins nestled in the valley along side a rushing creek.

Brian Armagost, the 29-year-old Chef of Barton Ridge Plantation and The Hateras Club, has always had a passion for cooking: "I remember that moment like it was yesterday. I guess it was about age four when my Grandmother sat me on the counter allowing me to help make her famous pear relish. Showing me exactly what went in her magic concoction sparked an interest that grew in me through the years."

Chef Armagost's professional career started at age 16 working in many restaurants in his home town of Montgomery, Alabama. "I would watch every television show and read everything I could get my hands on that pertained to the culinary arts. Cooking was truly in my heart."

After brief stints in Tuscaloosa and Birmingham, Alabama, Brian traveled to San Francisco, California, to gain more depth to his craft. There he worked at Windy City West and Sandi's Café as well as rounding for free in over 50 different restaurants in the bay area: "If there is one thing a chef cannot turn down, it is free help. I was more than willing to clean lettuce and chop parsley to see what the masters were doing. I was absolutely blown away! It was a remarkable learning experience."

Brian's love for the south soon brought him closer to home in Baton Rouge, Louisiana. There he took the position of Executive Sous Chef at Juban's Restaurant, a twenty-two-year staple of Creole and Cajun cuisine. Once again Brian resumed rounding many New Orleans restaurants. There, he claims, he felt like a fish in water: "In California I learned technique but in Louisiana I learned flavor. Everything just all of a sudden made sense to me. I feel Louisiana brought me into my own. I wanted to bring all this back to my roots and then I found Barton Ridge Plantation. Howard and Liz Barton offered the perfect platform to develop my own style of cooking."

Chef Armagost is in the forefront of New Southern Cuisine at Barton Ridge and at his new restaurant, The Hateras Club on the Gulf Coast. His combination of old southern ingredients with multicultural technique has spawned many new delights.

BARTON RIDGE PLANTATION

Crawfish, Pancetta and Tomato Bruschetta

1	(12-inch) French bread baguette
3	tablespoons olive oil, divided
1	large clove garlic
¼	cup pancetta bacon, diced
1	pound crawfish tail meat
2	tablespoons kalamata olives, diced
½	cup diced red onion
1	small green bell pepper, diced
1	teaspoon crushed red pepper
¼	cup dry sherry
	juice of ½ lemon
½	cup diced Roma tomatoes
1	tablespoon chopped fresh oregano
2	tablespoons butter
3	cups shredded Boston, Bibb and Radicchio lettuces
½	cup shaved Asiago cheese

- Cut bread into 1½-inch thick slices at a sharp angle. Brush with 2 tablespoons olive oil. Grill over medium flame on each side until toasted but not burned. Remove from grill and rub briskly with garlic clove. Set aside and keep warm.

- Heat 1 tablespoon olive oil in a medium pan and saute pancetta over medium-high heat until slightly brown. Add crawfish, olives, onion, bell pepper and crushed pepper. Cook until onions become transparent. Add sherry, lemon juice, tomatoes and oregano. Let simmer 2 to 3 minutes. Remove from heat and swirl in butter. Salt to taste.

- Place bread on plate over lettuce mixture. Top with crawfish mixture and sprinkle with cheese. Serves 6.

BARTON RIDGE PLANTATION

Field Pea, Tomato & Buffalo Mozzarella Salad

3 cups cooked fresh field peas
12 strips bacon, cooked crisp and crumbled
1 small red onion, julienned
sliced, fresh jalapeño, optional
2 tablespoons julienned fresh basil
1 cup olive oil
¾ cup red wine vinegar
2 tablespoons soy sauce
½ cup firmly packed brown sugar
salt and pepper
1 teaspoon crushed red pepper
3 Beefsteak or Better Boy tomatoes
1 tablespoon chopped fresh oregano
1 pound fresh buffalo mozzarella

- Combine field peas, bacon, red onion, basil, olive oil, vinegar, soy sauce, brown sugar, salt to taste and pepper in a mixing bowl. Add jalapeño if a spicier salad is desired. Let rest at room temperature for at least 1 hour.

- Slice tomatoes about an eighth of an inch thick. Sprinkle with salt, pepper and oregano. Set aside.

- Slice cheese into eighth-inch slices.

- To assemble, place tomatoes in an overlapping circle around plate. Top with a scoop of field pea mixture and circle with sliced cheese. Spoon around liquid from field pea mixture. Garnish with a sprig of oregano. Serves 6.

BARTON RIDGE PLANTATION

Andouille Sausage and Sweet Potato Soup

2 large sweet potatoes, peeled and halved
½ pound andouille sausage
10 cloves garlic
olive oil
1 small yellow onion, minced
2 stalks celery, minced
1 small red bell pepper, minced
2 tablespoons chopped fresh thyme
1 tablespoon cracked black pepper
3 cups chicken stock
1 cup whipping cream
cayenne pepper to taste

- Preheat oven to 375 degrees. Place sweet potato, sausage and garlic on a baking sheet. Bake 20 minutes. Remove sausage and garlic. Continue baking potatoes until soft, about 20 more minutes. Remove from oven and place in a food processor with garlic. Puree until smooth.

- Cut sausage into bite-size pieces and set aside.

- Heat olive oil over medium heat in a sauce pot until almost smoking. Add onions, celery, bell pepper, thyme and cracked pepper. Saute until onions are slightly brown. Add chicken stock, cream, the sweet potato puree, sausage and cayenne pepper to taste.

- Bring to a simmer over low heat and cook for 30 minutes to combine flavors.

BARTON RIDGE PLANTATION

Chilled Avocado, Tomato and Silver Queen Corn Soup

- 2 tablespoons salt
- 3 ears silver queen corn, shucked and cleaned
- 2 medium beefsteak tomatoes, peeled, seeded and diced
- ¼ cup chopped fresh cilantro
- 3 large ripe avocados
- 1 medium onion, chopped
- 1 jalapeño, seeded
- juice of 1 lemon
- 2 cups chicken stock
- 1 cup heavy cream
- salt and cracked pepper
- dark chili powder

- Fill a 6-quart pot halfway with water. Add 2 tablespoons salt. Bring to a boil over high heat. Drop in corn and cook 3 minutes. Remove corn and shock in ice water. Cut kernels from cobs with a sharp knife. Reserve cobs.

- Combine corn, tomatoes and cilantro in a small bowl. Season with salt and pepper to taste. Refrigerate.

- Hold corn cobs standing on end over a shallow dish and scrape juice and pulp off cob with a knife. Reserve.

- Cut avocados in half, remove pits and scoop out meat with a spoon.

- Combine avocado, corn juice, jalapeño, onion, lemon juice and chicken stock in food process or blender and puree until smooth. Pour mixture through a small sieve into a mixing bowl. Whisk cream into mixture and season to taste with salt and pepper. Cover and refrigerate for at least one hour.

- To serve, pour soup into chilled bowls. Top with a large dollop of corn/tomato mixture and garnish with chili powder.

BARTON RIDGE PLANTATION

Gulf Oysters and Tasso Ham over Fried Green Tomatoes

4	firm, green tomatoes, thinly sliced
2	cups buttermilk
1	egg, lightly beaten
1	teaspoon hot pepper sauce
1	tablespoon olive oil
½	cup diced yellow onion
8	ounces tasso ham, diced
½	cup diced bell pepper
2	(6-inch) sprigs fresh rosemary
2	bay leaves
2	tablespoons minced garlic
2	teaspoons cracked black pepper
2	teaspoons crushed red pepper
½	cup beer
1	pint oysters, drained and liquid reserved
2	large beefsteak tomatoes, peeled, seeded and diced
2	tablespoons tomato paste
1	tablespoon Worcestershire sauce

juice of 1 lemon
4 tablespoons butter
salt
1 cup all-purpose flour
1 cup corn meal
peanut oil
chopped fresh chives
grated Parmesan cheese

- Lightly salt tomatoes and place in a shallow bowl. Combine buttermilk, egg and hot pepper sauce and pour over tomatoes. Soak for 30 minutes.

- While tomatoes are soaking, heat olive oil in a large saute pan until almost smoking. Add onions, ham, bell pepper, rosemary, bay leaves, garlic, black and red pepper. Saute until onions are translucent and lightly browned. Deglaze pan with beer and reserved liquid from oysters. Add tomatoes, tomato paste, Worcestershire sauce and lemon juice. Bring to a boil and reduce by half. Add oysters and cook five minutes. Remove from heat and whisk in butter. Add salt to taste.

- Remove tomatoes from buttermilk soak and dredge in a mixture of the flour and cornmeal. Heat peanut oil in a skillet to 350 degrees. Fry tomatoes until crisp, 2 to 3 minutes. Drain on paper towels.

- To serve, arrange tomatoes in an overlapping circle. Top with Oyster Stew and garnish with chives and Parmesan.

BARTON RIDGE PLANTATION

Sesame and Peanut-Crusted Soft Shell Crab on Spinach Chiffonade with Creole Horseradish Cream and Tamarind-Orange Infusion

Tamarind-Orange Infusion:

½	cup orange marmalade
1	tablespoon tamarind paste
1	jalapeño, diced
2	green onions, chopped
1	tablespoon pickled ginger, chopped
1	clove garlic, minced
1	tablespoon rice wine vinegar

juice of 1 lemon

Creole Horseradish Cream:

1	cup whipping cream
1	tablespoon prepared horseradish
1	tablespoon creole mustard

salt

Soft Shell:

salt and pepper

6	jumbo soft shell crabs, cleaned
1	large egg
1	teaspoon hot pepper sauce
1	cup all-purpose flour
½	cup dry roasted peanuts, crushed
¼	cup black sesame seeds
1	bunch spinach, washed and cut into thin strips

- For Infusion: Combine all ingredients and mix well. Refrigerate at least 30 minutes to combine flavors.

- For Creole Horseradish Cream: Combine all ingredients in a saucepan. Bring to a boil over high heat. Reduce heat and simmer 2 minutes.

- For Soft Shell: Heat peanut oil in a cast iron Dutch oven to 350 degrees.

- Salt and pepper crabs to taste and set aside.

- Whisk 1 cup water, egg and hot pepper sauce together in a bowl. Combine flour, sesame seeds, peanuts and salt and pepper to taste in another bowl.

- Dip crabs in egg wash, then in flour mixture. Place in hot oil and fry for 3 to 4 minutes. Drain on paper towels.

- To assemble: Place a small pile of spinach in center of plate. Spoon Creole Horseradish Cream around and over spinach. Place a crab on top of spinach. Finish by spooning a large dollop of infusion on crab. Serve immediately.

BARTON RIDGE PLANTATION

Grilled Quail with Smoked Gouda Grits and Tomato Gravy

12 quail
salt and pepper
½ cup olive oil
½ cup Worcestershire sauce
½ cup creole mustard
¼ cup balsamic vinegar
¼ cup firmly packed brown sugar
2 tablespoons soy sauce
3 cups half-and-half, divided
3 cups chicken stock or bouillon, divided
1 cup quick grits (not instant)
4 ounce smoked gouda cheese or cheese of your choice, grated
4 slices bacon, diced
1 small onion, diced
1 clove garlic, minced
1 cup Madeira wine
3 large tomatoes, peeled, seeded, diced and drained or 1 (10-ounce) can diced tomatoes
4 tablespoons butter
diced green onions

- Dress and clean quail, being sure to remove all shot. Rinse with cold water, pat dry and season with salt and pepper to taste. Combine olive oil, Worcestershire sauce, mustard, vinegar, brown sugar and soy sauce. Place quail in this marinade, cover and refrigerate at least 2 hours, turning frequently.

- While quail are marinating, start and clean grill. A gas grill will do, but I prefer charcoal with a handful of dry hickory wood thrown on right when you fire the birds.

- Bring 2 cups half-and-half and 2 cups chicken stock to a boil. Add grits, stirring constantly until mixture thickens. Add cheese, cover and set aside.

- Saute bacon, onions and garlic in a medium sauce pot until onion is translucent. Deglaze pan with wine and remaining 1 cup stock. Stir in remaining half-and-half. Reduce by half and add tomatoes. Bring to a boil, remove from heat and swirl in butter.

- Remove quail from marinade, reserving marinade. Place quail on grill and cook about 8 minutes, turning and basting with marinade every 2 minutes.

- To serve, put one cup of grits on plate. Top with 2 quail and finish with tomato gravy. Garnish with green onions and serve. Serves 6.

BARTON RIDGE PLANTATION

Stewed Rabbit and Shiitake Mushrooms on Crispy Yukon Potato Hash Cakes

Potato Hash Cakes:
1	tablespoon salt
12	yukon gold potatoes, shredded (6 cups)
½	cup chopped green onion
2	cloves garlic, minced
1	large egg
¼	cup sour cream
¼	cup milk
1	teaspoon hot pepper sauce
1	sleeve round, buttery crackers, crushed
½	cup melted butter

Rabbit:
2	teaspoons freshly ground pepper
2	teaspoons kosher salt
2	teaspoons sugar
2	teaspoons whole dried thyme
1	small rabbit, quartered
¼	cup olive oil
½	cup all-purpose flour
1	cup Marsala wine
3	slices bacon, diced
½	pound shiitake mushrooms, stems removed and julienned
1	yellow onion, julienned
1	stalk celery, diced
	freshly ground black pepper
1	large tomato, peeled, seeded and diced
1	tablespoon chopped parsley
8	leaves fresh basil, finely sliced

- For Hash Cakes: Fill a 4-quart sauce pot half way with cold water and add salt. Bring to a boil over high heat. Add potatoes and cook until potatoes have a soft bite, 3 to 5 minutes.

- Drain in a colander and pour into a large mixing bowl. Add green onion, garlic, egg, sour cream, milk and hot pepper sauce. Mix until all ingredients are well incorporated. Cool for about 20 minutes.

- Form potato mixture into 16 round cakes about 1 inch thick. Coat each cake well with cracker crumbs and refrigerate.

- For Rabbit: Mix pepper, salt, sugar and thyme. Rub into rabbit. Heat olive oil in a large cast iron skillet over medium heat. Coat rabbit well with flour and place in skillet. Brown well on all sides. Remove rabbit, reserving drippings.

- Place rabbit in a small pot with Marsala and just enough water to cover. Bring to a boil over high heat. Reduce heat to medium-low, cover and cook 30 minutes.

- While rabbit is cooking, add bacon, mushrooms, onion, celery and pepper to the drippings in the skillet. Saute until onions are translucent. Turn off heat.

- Remove rabbit from pot and pull meat from bone. Reserve meat and return bones to cooking liquid. Bring liquid back to a boil and reduce by half.

- Strain rabbit stock and add to mushroom mixture along with meat, tomatoes and parsley. Heat mixture and simmer.

- Preheat oven to 375 degrees.

- Place cooled potato cakes on a buttered baking sheet, spacing evenly. Coat well with melted butter and bake 10 to 12 minutes.

- To assemble, place 2 potato cakes on a plate. Spoon rabbit stew over cakes and around plate. Garnish with basil.

BARTON RIDGE PLANTATION

Location Map

Barton Ridge Plantation is located approximately one hour from the Birmingham, Alabama, Airport; 2.5 hours from the Atlanta International Airport; and one hour from the Alexander City Airport. Limousine service is available to and from these airports.

Route 2, Box 105A
Rockford, AL 35136

Reservations

Barton Ridge Plantation offers exceptional amenities and hunters are encouraged to bring their spouses. Barton Ridge is designed to entertain non-hunters as well as hunters. Antique shopping and championship golf are nearby with limousine service provided. Prices available upon request. Their facilities include scenic hiking trails, sparkling swimming pool, and tennis courts.

Barton Ridge is confident that you will find, as so many others have, that their chef, impeccable service, and accommodations are unparalleled.

For reservations, call toll free:
(877) 396-8004 or 1-800-953-7330

Reservation Hours
8:00 a.m. through 5:00 p.m.
Monday through Saturday

Barton Ridge Plantation is open year round for corporate retreats and company meetings. Their corporate facilities include lodging, office machines, meeting rooms, and a wide variety of outdoor events. Contact Barton Ridge Plantation today for details.

Bostick Plantation

History

The Bostick family is only one of 200 families that still maintain original royal tracts. They have spent the last 10 years working with wildlife experts to enhance habitat and manage the growing population of trophy game. The end result has been highly successful, producing one of the finest commercial hunting facilities in the south while keeping the Bostick tradition of comfortable hunting and down-home South Carolina hospitality.

Upon your arrival at the Plantation, you will get the feeling of having been dropped back in time. Your lodge will be a rustic farmhouse originally used by the family during the early plantation era. The old homestead comfortably holds 10–15 hunters. All around the lodge are expanses of bean and cornfields, rye patches, hardwoods, and swamp bottoms which make up the carefully managed habitat for trophy game. Whether your tastes run to whitetail deer, quail, wild turkey or Russian boar, a comfortable lodge and a good night's rest await you.

Bostick Plantation is not as remotely located as it may seem. Located in the southeastern portion of South Carolina and bordering the Savannah River, they are only 10 miles from Estill and just 50 miles north of Savannah, Georgia.

Quail Hunting

Bostick Plantation has spent the last 10 years working with wildlife experts to enhance habitat and manage the ever growing population of quail. Unlike many preserves, Bostick Plantation offers you the opportunity to hunt both wild and pen-raised birds. And, for many who have never experienced a wild covey rise, it is an experience not soon forgotten.

Unlike other licensed preserves who specialize in only pen-raised quail, Bostick has extended their program, ever mindful of the tradition of wild birds. Their participation with wildlife experts has led to the development of quail raised for fast-flying, hard-shooting enjoyment. They stock birds before the season and often during the season to maintain a large covey rise. It is not uncommon to flush a truly wild covey from 200-year-old stock, followed by a covey of their own special breed of birds. Naturally, Bostick's attention to careful habitat maintenance, good cover, and seed crops ensures your successful hunt.

Bostick Plantation has discovered that the best experience come from a mixture of a casual ride through their rolling country side and careful walk-ups on coveys. For that reason they have developed their own specially equipped jeeps with high rear seats, padded gun rack, and dog boxes. You get a panoramic view of the countryside, and the dogs work from a special vantage point.

Bostick's kennels are stocked with dogs that will adjust to almost any style of hunting, whether you choose to walk or spend more time riding. Since many of you share pride in training and working your own fine hunting dog, they are welcome at Bostick Plantation. Just give Bostick Plantation a call in advance and they'll arrange for their full participation.

Bow Hunting

Bostick Plantation has 1,500 acres of land available for your bow hunting pleasure. No guns or rifles are allowed in this area. We have our own permanent archery stand available for you, but you may bring your own climber if you choose. Our guides will assist you in placing your climber. Some Bostick stands are fed with our famous Bostick *"Buck Buckets."*

Deer Hunting

All game is truly wild at Bostick Plantation. There are no fences restricting the movement of animals on their land. Official state surveys demonstrate the buck-to-doe ratio to be about one buck for every 1.8 does. With their guests' cooperation, Bostick's highly successful trophy buck program protects young bucks, the four to six pointers, to ensure the visiting sportsman a chance to shoot a true trophy.

Bostick Plantation's management techniques are state-of-the-art. Hundreds of acres planted in corn and soybeans guarantee plenty of available food for game. In areas not under general farming, Bostick Plantation plants peas and rye. The more food available, the greater accumulation of deer.

Deer stands have been erected at proven high performance locations where those big 10 and 12-point trophies are likely to frequent. Bostick Plantation stands have been constructed with hunter comfort, safety, and concealment in mind. Their stands are made of steel, either free-standing or leaners. All sides are covered with camouflage, and there is a seat in the middle for your favorite cushion.

Turkey Hunting

Turkey hunting is unlike most hunting because it is a one-on-one situation. When that big old boss gobbler is cock of the roost, you are faced with a challenge that is unlike any that you have ever experienced. He is unpredictable in just about everything he does. There is no way to describe the excitement you feel when that old gobbler is gobbling his head off and you are sitting—waiting and hoping he will fly down in your direction. Give him that low tree yelp. Will he ever fly down? Maybe! He may choose to come right to you or at times he may come to rest two or three hundred yards away.

Of one thing you can be sure, turkey hunting is a sport of great challenge, patience, practice and a lot of desire to outwit that wise old gobbler. In all my years of turkey hunting, I have had only one turkey come to me within minutes of the time I had set up and began calling. Bostick Plantation does their best to supply you with the memories of a lifetime in taking that wily old bird.

Boar Hunting

Bostick Plantation has the best hog hunting in the South. Russian boar flourish in our ancient plantation swamps. These hogs are the offspring of Russian boars imported by our ancestors and released at Bostick several generations back. These boar are tough, gamey and exciting to hunt. They populate the many swamp and river bottoms that form part of the Savannah River watershed bordering Bostick Plantation.

These hogs are smart and have adapted to the wild so successfully to allow Bostick Plantation bragging rights to one of the largest boar-to-acre ratios in the entire southeast. Our wildlife management program has resulted in boars that tip the scales at 300 pounds.

BOSTICK PLANTATION

Asparagus Casserole

1 can cream of mushroom soup
1 can mushrooms, drained
1 tablespoon chopped pimiento
2 heaping tablespoons sour cream
2 cans asparagus, drained
saltines, crumbled
1 tablespoon margarine

- Combine soup, mushrooms, pimiento and sour cream. Spread a layer of mixture in bottom of a greased casserole dish. Top with a layer of asparagus. Continue layering.

- Top with cracker crumbs and margarine. Bake in a preheated 350 degree oven until bubbly.

Glorious Macaroni

¼ cup diced onion
1 jar pimientos, drained
2 tablespoons butter
1 pound grated cheese
1 can cream of mushroom soup
1 jar mushrooms, drained
1 (8-ounce) box sea shell macaroni, cooked according to package directions and drained

- Sauté onion and pimientos in melted butter until tender. Combine with remaining ingredients and pour into a greased casserole dish.

- Bake in a preheated 325 degree oven for 45 minutes to 1 hour.

Potato Casserole

1 (2-pound) bag frozen hash browns
½ cup melted butter
1 teaspoon salt
1 teaspoon pepper
½ cup chopped onion
1 pint sour cream
1 cup grated cheese
¾ cup crushed corn flakes

- Combine all ingredients except corn flakes. Pour into a greased 9 x 13-inch baking dish. Top with corn flakes.

- Bake in a preheated 350 degree oven for 15 to 20 minutes.

Hot Pineapple Casserole

1	large can crushed pineapple in natural juices
½	cup butter, melted
4	slices bread, torn in bite-size pieces
⅔	cup sugar
3	eggs, lightly beaten
1	tablespoon flour

- Spread pineapple in a greased casserole dish. Top with butter and bread pieces. Mix to combine. Add sugar, eggs and flour and mix again.

- Bake, uncovered, in a preheated 350 degree oven for 30 to 40 minutes. Do not brown. Serves 6.

Incredible Crab Soup

¼	cup finely chopped onion
6	tablespoons butter or margarine
2	tablespoons all-purpose flour
2	(12-ounce) packages frozen crab meat, thawed, or 1½ pounds fresh crab meat
1	teaspoon salt
⅛	teaspoon pepper
1	quart plus 2 cups milk
1	cup whipping cream
½	cup Scotch whiskey

chopped parsley

- Sauté onion in butter until tender. Add flour and cook 1 minute, stirring constantly. Add crab meat, salt and pepper. Cook over low heat for 10 minutes, stirring occasionally.

- Gradually add milk, stirring. Cook over low heat 15 minutes. Add cream and Scotch. Stir well. Garnish with parsley.

Pork Chop Casserole

6-8 pork chops
salt and pepper
1 can cream of mushroom soup
¼ cup water
pinch of thyme
pinch of parsley
1 cup sour cream
1 can fried onion rings

- Season pork chops with salt and pepper to taste. Brown in hot oil, drain and place in a baking dish.

- Combine soup and water in a small saucepan. Heat and add thyme and parsley. Remove from heat and stir in sour cream. Pour over chops.

- Cover and bake in a preheated 350 degree oven for 1 hour. Remove cover and top with onion rings. Bake, uncovered, for 5 more minutes.

Braised Venison Steaks

cubed venison steaks
salt and pepper
flour
1 can cream of mushroom soup
1 soup can water

- Preheat oven to 500 degrees.

- Season steaks to taste and dredge in flour. Fry in hot grease until done.

- Remove steaks to a 9 x 13-inch glass baking dish. Combine soup and water and pour over steaks. Cover tightly with foil.

- Bake for 10 minutes, then turn oven off. Leave meat in oven for 1½ to 2 hours.

BOSTICK PLANTATION

Lodging

At Bostick Plantation a comfortable lodge and a good night's rest will await you. A warm glowing fireplace in the old living room soothes the chill of the early fall evening while you await the specialties of a low country supper highlighting the days' successful hunt.

So if you want to experience the best that Bostick has to offer,
call their toll free number

1-800-542-6913

P.O. Box 728
Estill, SC 29918
www.bostickplantation.com

Deer Hunting
August 15 – January 1

Quail Hunting
November 15 – March 15

Turkey Hunting
March 15 – May 1

Russian Boar Hunting
Year-round

BOSTICK PLANTATION

BOSTICK PLANTATION

Shrimp Victoria

1 pound fresh shrimp, peeled and deveined
1 small onion, finely chopped
¼ cup butter or margarine
1 (6-ounce) can mushrooms, drained
1 tablespoon flour
¼ teaspoon salt
dash of cayenne pepper
1 cup sour cream
1½ cups cooked rice

- Sauté shrimp and onion in butter until shrimp turn pink. Add mushrooms and cook 5 minutes. Sprinkle with flour, salt and pepper. Stir in sour cream and cook on low 10 minutes, stirring frequently. Do not allow mixture to boil.

- Serve over rice. Serves 4 to 6.

Baked Quail

quail
salt and pepper
flour
1 onion, sliced
butter

- Season quail to taste. Dredge in flour and brown in hot fat. Remove to a baking dish.

- Sauté onion in melted butter until tender. Add to quail. Cover and bake in a preheated 350 degree oven until tender, 2 to 3 hours.

BOSTICK PLANTATION

Lodging

At Bostick Plantation a comfortable lodge and a good night's rest will await you. A warm glowing fireplace in the old living room soothes the chill of the early fall evening while you await the specialties of a low country supper highlighting the days' successful hunt.

So if you want to experience the best that Bostick has to offer,
call their toll free number

1-800-542-6913

P.O. Box 728
Estill, SC 29918
www.bostickplantation.com

Deer Hunting
August 15 – January 1

Quail Hunting
November 15 – March 15

Turkey Hunting
March 15 – May 1

Russian Boar Hunting
Year-round

The Lodge at Cabin Bluff

The Lodge at Cabin Bluff

One of the earliest hunting and fishing clubs in America, The Lodge at Cabin Bluff is steeped in history. Overlooking the Cumberland River, across from the famed Cumberland Island National Seashore, Cabin Bluff is located in southeast Georgia, an area long known for its exceptional hunting and fishing.

First inhabited by the Timucuan Indians, the area was successively explored and settled by French colonists in 1562, the Spanish in 1565, and then the English in 1742.

By 1800, Revolutionary hero Charles Floyd had created Belleview Plantation there, followed by his son, John, who had his own plantation, Fairfield.

Following the plantation era, Cabin Bluff was home to what may have been the first hunting club in America. The Camden Hunt Club, which had a national reputation for superb hunting, was organized in 1827. A strict code of conduct governed the club. According to its rigid regulations, members were to meet twice a month, and any member not in attendance would be fined.

In 1927, Hudson Motor Car Company magnate and Sea Island Company founder Howard Coffin bought Cabin Bluff, making many improvements to the land and hunting lodge to recapture the mood of the old hunt club. The next year, President Calvin Coolidge hunted at Cabin Bluff during his visit with Coffin at The Cloister, Sea Island. Soon afterward, Coffin hosted some of the most influential newspaper and magazine publishers of the day, and Cabin Bluff was used by many guests of The Cloister for over a decade.

The property was sold in 1942, but Sea Island reacquired interest in the property and assumed responsibility for the lodge and recreational facilities in a joint ownership arrangement with Mead Corporation.

The same rustic seclusion of the early days of Cabin Bluff remains. Today its rustic charm, privacy, and extraordinary surrounding natural resources combine to offer some of the best opportunities for sportsmen anywhere.

Lodging

Astonishing natural beauty. Exceptional sports and recreation. Rustic charm. Perfect serenity. Even these laudatory phrases fail to fully convey the allure that is the Cabin Bluff experience.

Overlooking Cumberland River, The Lodge at Cabin Bluff is surrounded by more than 100 square miles of timber preserve in Georgia's coastal lowlands. One of the earliest hunting and fishing clubs in America, The Lodge has the distinction of being endorsed by Orvis for both fly fishing and wing shooting. Its rustic charm, privacy, and extraordinary surrounding natural resources combine to offer one of the finest retreat facilities in North America—ideal for family reunions or corporate gatherings.

Season by season, only a handful of properties can match the scope of its services. An exceptional range of activities and sports are available to guests, most of which are included in each package. Accommodations, all meals, beverages, hunting, hiking, fishing (freshwater, dock and bluffs) sporting clays, and access to Cumberland Island as well as paddle tennis, shuffleboard, hiking and billiards, use of on-site pool facilities, jacuzzi, sauna, and exercise equipment are available for guest use.

Another activity available to guests is golf, uniquely crafted and perfectly suited to this premier retreat facility. Course designer Davis Love III has fashioned a layout that is immensely challenging and, with a keen stewardship to creative use of its 50 acres, a stroke of pure design genius.

Special arrangements may be made for kayaking, chartered fishing, horseback riding, waterway cruises on a vintage motor or sailing yacht, spa services, and sports instruction.

October through March, Cabin Bluff has some of the best deer hunting in the south, as well as turkey, quail, boar, and small game hunting. Knowledgeable guides lead parties through some of the 40,000 acres to ideal spots. The Lodge at Cabin Bluff comes into its own during wing season with some of the best wing shooting in the south.

Deep sea and river fishing are excellent with fishing challenges of every description. Bass and bream for freshwater, speckled trout, tarpon and redfish inshore, and king mackerel offshore.

Cabin Bluff has hosted many hunting and fishing excursions over the years, as well as family reunions. The natural surroundings invite guests to immerse themselves in its simple, uncomplicated pleasures. It has also served as the site for numerous corporate gatherings as well.

Dining

The Lodge at Cabin Bluff accommodates groups of up to 32 persons with three and six-day packages available. The main lodge and six cabins give guests plenty of flexibility in planning room arrangements, providing 16 private rooms with private baths. The rooms reflect a rustic elegance much in character with Cabin Bluff's history and natural beauty. Meals are a hearty fare with home-style breakfasts, mid-day meals, riverside oyster roasts, and open-air cookouts.

Menus from The Lodge at Cabin Bluff

Cocktails Served in the Main Lodge

Dinner Served in the Pub

Roast Prime Rib of Beef & Crab Cakes or Grilled Catch of the Day
Tossed Salad with Choice of Dressing
Garlic Mashed Potatoes or Steamed Rice with Pan Gravy
Seasoned Green Beans
Baked Yellow Squash Casserole
Homemade Buttermilk Biscuits
Pecan Pie

Breakfast Served in the Dining Hall

Fresh Seasonal Fruit
Soft Scrambled Eggs   Baked Grits Soufflé
Grilled Sausage Links   Crisp Country Bacon
Homemade Biscuits
Breakfast Beverages

Lunch Served in the Dining Hall

Tossed Green Salad
Bean Soup with Onions, Peppers, Ham & Rice
Sandwich Tray with Turkey and Roast Beef
Strawberry Shortcake
Lunch Beverages

Dinner Served in the Pub

Roasted Pork Loin & Baked Cornish Hen
Tossed Salad with Choice of Dressing
Wild Rice   Homestyle Gravy
Fresh Buttered Carrots   Mustard and Turnip Greens
Homemade Biscuits
Blueberry Crunch with Ice Cream
Dinner Beverages

THE LODGE AT CABIN BLUFF

Smothered Quail

12 (4 to 6-ounce) quail
salt
3 tablespoons all-purpose flour
½-1 cup canola cooking oil
1 cup finely chopped onion
1 cup shredded carrots
1 cup chicken broth
1½ cups half-and-half or whipping cream
½ cup white wine
1 cup sliced fresh mushrooms
1-2 tablespoons oil

- Sprinkle insides of quail lightly with salt. Dust outsides with flour.

- Heat oil in a 4-quart saucepan or Dutch oven. Brown quail on all sides. Drain off excess oil and reduce heat. Sprinkle onion and carrots over quail.

- Combine broth, cream and wine and pour over quail. Cover and bake in a preheated 350 degree oven for 1½ hours. Remove cover and bake 30 minutes more, basting with sauce three times.

- During the last half hour of baking, lightly Sauté mushrooms in oil. Drain and add to quail. Continue cooking for 15 minutes. Serves 6.

Cabin Bluff Wild Rice

1 cup wild rice
4 cups water
½ teaspoon salt
4 slices bacon or 2 slices thick-sliced bacon
1 medium onion, sliced

- Place rice in a strainer and wash thoroughly under running water. Combine rice, water and salt in a large saucepan. Bring to a boil, reduce heat, cover and boil gently until rice is nearly tender, about 40 minutes. Do not overcook.

- Drain rice in a colander and let stand 1 hour.

- Cook bacon in a large skillet until crisp. Drain, crumble and set aside. Reserve 1 tablespoon bacon drippings and discard the rest. Sauté onion in reserved drippings until tender but not brown.

- Add rice and bacon to skillet. Cook over low heat, stirring occasionally, until rice is heated through and flavors are blended. Serves 3 to 4.

THE LODGE AT CABIN BLUFF

Crab Cakes with Dill Sauce

1 green onion, finely chopped
1 clove garlic, pressed
2 tablespoons finely chopped red bell pepper
1 tablespoon butter
cayenne pepper
3 tablespoons whipping cream
1 tablespoon Dijon mustard
1 egg, lightly beaten
½ teaspoon minced parsley
1 cup bread crumbs, divided
1 pound fresh white or claw crab meat, picked through for shells
¼ cup grated Parmesan cheese
2 tablespoons olive oil
2 tablespoons butter

Dill Sauce
1 cup mayonnaise
¼ cup buttermilk
2 tablespoons chopped fresh dill
1 tablespoon minced fresh parsley
2 teaspoons lemon juice
1 tablespoon grated lemon rind
1 clove garlic, minced

- Sauté onion, garlic and bell pepper in butter until onion is translucent. Remove form heat and add cayenne, cream and mustard. Stir in egg, parsley and ½ cup bread crumbs. Blend well. Gently mix in crab meat.

- Divide mixture into eight ½-inch thick patties. Combine remaining bread crumbs and Parmesan cheese. Press lightly on both sides of the cakes.

- Combine all ingredients and chill until mixture thickens. Garnish each crab cake with a spoonful.

- Cover and refrigerate until firm, about 2 hours. Place on a greased baking sheet and drizzle with oil and butter. Bake in a preheated 400 degree oven 7 to 10 minutes. Serve with Dill Sauce.

Shrimp Creole

1½ pounds fresh shrimp in shells
2 tablespoons olive or canola oil
½ cup coarsely chopped celery
½ cup coarsely chopped onion
½ cup coarsely chopped green bell pepper
2 cups chopped tomatoes
2 tablespoons minced parsley
½ teaspoon paprika
1 large bay leaf
⅛ teaspoon crushed red pepper
⅛ teaspoon dried thyme, crumbled
½ teaspoon hot pepper sauce
salt and pepper

- Bring a large pot of salted water to a boil. Add shrimp and return to a boil. Reduce heat and simmer until shrimp turn pink, 2 to 3 minutes. Drain, peel and devein.

- Heat oil in a 2-quart saucepan. Sauté celery, onion and bell pepper until tender but not brown. Add tomatoes, parsley, paprika, bay leaf, red pepper, thyme and hot pepper sauce. Simmer, uncovered, until the desired consistency, 10 to 15 minutes. Discard bay leaf.

- Add shrimp to sauce and heat just until hot. Season to taste with salt and pepper. Serves 3 to 4.

Broiled Speckled Trout

¼ cup fresh lemon juice
1 tablespoon oil
½ teaspoon Worcestershire sauce
dash of hot pepper sauce
1½ pounds trout fillets with skin on
salt and pepper to taste

- Combine lemon juice, oil, Worcestershire and hot pepper sauce.

- Place fillets, skin-side-up, on broiler pan. Brush with lemon juice mixture. Season with salt and pepper. Broil 3 to 4 inches from heat source until skin bubbles, about 4 minutes.

- Turn fillets, brush with marinade and sprinkle with salt and pepper. Broil until fish flakes easily with a fork, 6 to 8 minutes. Brush with remaining marinade and serve immediately.

THE LODGE AT CABIN BLUFF

Mixed Salad with Ginger Vinaigrette

2 tablespoons fresh lemon juice
¼ cup olive oil
1 clove garlic, minced
½ teaspoon salt
½ teaspoon sugar
½ teaspoon grated lemon rind
½ teaspoon grated fresh ginger
mixed salad greens
sliced green and red bell peppers
sliced fresh pears
pine nuts
freshly grated Parmesan cheese

- Combine lemon juice, olive oil, garlic, salt, sugar, lemon rind and ginger in a covered container. Shake well to blend.

- Place greens in a salad bowl and top with bell pepper slices, pears and pine nuts. Pour vinaigrette over salad and toss to coat. Garnish with Parmesan.

Zesty Lemon Sesame Broccoli

3 pounds broccoli
2 tablespoons minced garlic
⅔ cup fresh lemon juice
2 tablespoons sesame seeds, lightly toasted

- Trim broccoli florets and cut into small pieces. Peel stems and slice into thin rounds.

- Steam broccoli in a vegetable steamer until it turns bright green and is slightly tender, about 4 minutes. Drain and place in a salad bowl.

- Combine garlic and lemon juice. Pour over broccoli and toss to coat. Sprinkle with sesame seeds. Serve immediately to preserve color. Serves 6 to 8.

THE LODGE AT CABIN BLUFF

Baked Apple Pudding with Brandy Sauce

6	tablespoons butter, softened
1	cup sugar
1	teaspoon vanilla
1	egg
1	cup all-purpose flour
1	teaspoon baking soda
¼	teaspoon salt
¼	teaspoon ground nutmeg
2	cups grated, unpeeled tart green apples
½	cup chopped pecans

- Place butter in a mixing bowl and beat on medium speed for 30 seconds. Add sugar and vanilla and mix until well blended. Add egg and beat for 1 minute.

- Combine flour, soda, salt and nutmeg. Add to butter mixture, beating on low speed until combined. Stir in apples and pecans.

- Turn mixture into a lightly greased 8-inch square baking pan. Bake in a preheated 350 degree oven until done, 40 to 45 minutes. Serve warm or cold with Brandy Sauce. Serves 8 to 10.

Brandy Sauce

¼	cup butter, softened
1	cup powdered sugar
2	tablespoons brandy
1	teaspoon hot water
dash of salt	

- Beat butter and powdered sugar in a small mixing bowl until smooth. Add brandy, hot water and salt. Beat until fluffy. Serve immediately or chill. Yields ⅔ cup sauce.

Lemon Sugar Cookies

½	cup butter, softened
¼	cup vegetable shortening
1	cup sugar
¼	teaspoon lemon extract
1	egg, room temperature
2¼	cups all-purpose flour

- Preheat oven to 375 degrees.

- Combine butter, shortening, sugar and lemon extract in a large mixing bowl until well-blended and fluffy. Add egg and beat well. Gradually add flour, beating on low speed after each addition until just moistened.

- Drop by rounded teaspoonfuls onto an ungreased cookie sheet. Press with fork tines to flatter. Bake until lightly browned, about 10 minutes.

THE LODGE AT CABIN BLUFF

How to reach Cabin Bluff

Southbound on I-95
Approximately 34 miles south of Brunswick, Georgia, on I-95. Exit at Harrietts Bluff Road (exit 3) then turn left; go east 9.3 miles to Cabin Bluff gate on right.

From Florida, northbound on I-95
Approximately 27 miles north of Jacksonville International Airport on I-95. Exit at Harrietts Bluff Road (exit 3), then turn right; go east 9.3 miles to Cabin Bluff gate on right.

From Gate to Lodge
Turn right off Harrietts Bluff Rd. Go 1.3 miles; turn right. Go 1/2 mile; take first left.

Cabin Bluff Airfield
North 30 degrees 52 min
West 81 degrees 31.45 min

30.9 North, 81.6 West
28½ miles on 200 radial off
St. Simons Island

Grass field, 3000 feet long
West approach 2000 feet
East approach unlimited
Width including buffer, 200 feet

Intracoastal Waterway Access
Arrival by motor yacht is easily accommodated at our waterway docks. Advance arrangements recommended.

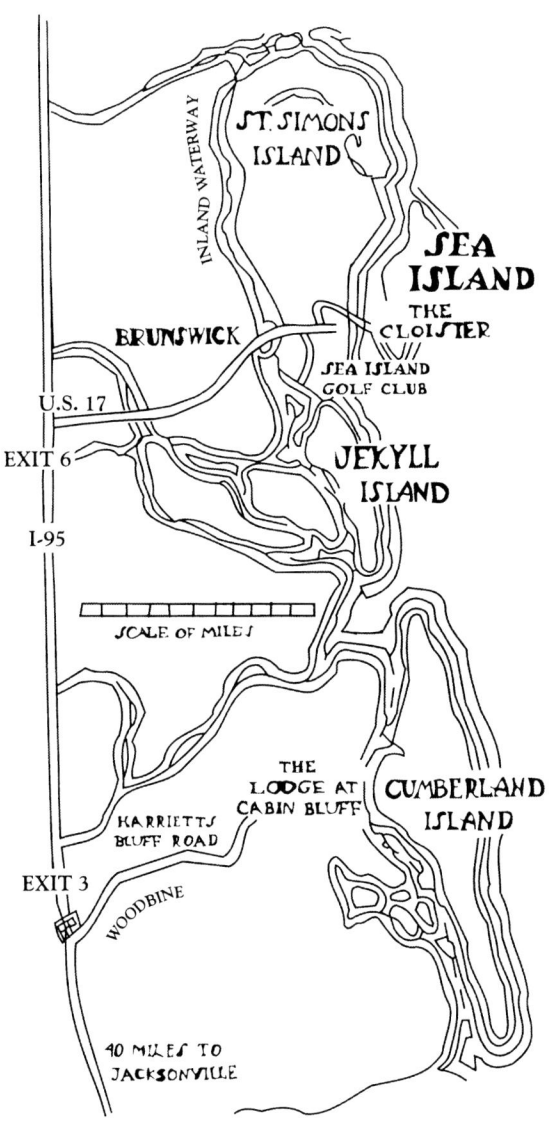

For information call

1-800-732-4752

or write

The Lodge at Cabin Bluff
P.O. Box 30203
Sea Island, GA 31561

Enon Plantation

Enon Plantation is located in the gentle rolling hills of Bullock County, Alabama. This southeastern portion of the state exemplifies the state slogan of "Alabama the Beautiful." Noted as one of the best hunting areas in the country and teaming with wildlife, nature is at its best at Enon. The word "Enon" is a biblical term meaning "land of much water" or "land of many springs." After 80 years of private ownership and dedication to extraordinary quail shooting, the Lord has blessed this land because of the splendor of its rolling pine forest, the expansive grandeur of its bottom land, and the quiet beauty of its lakes. Teaming with wild life, the land beckons to be explored and then return to the world a little wiser and a lot closer to God.

Enon Plantation's "Big House," built in the early 1900's has been lavishly and tastefully decorated for the comfort of guests. The huge "old meeting room" is the favorite gathering place and draws Enon's guests before as well as after a day of hunting. Its large fireplace and adjoining bar is the perfect setting for many tall tales. Delicious home-cooked meals are prepared and served by our courteous household staff who take great pride in taking care of Enon's guests.

Enon Plantation offers true plantation-style bobwhite quail hunting to avid wingshooters. Intense game management produces the type of hunt their guests enjoy and expect. Horseback hunts with a mule-drawn wagon or jeep hunts offer guests the options of their preferred style of hunting. Enon also offers liberated bird hunts which some people prefer.

Enon Plantation offers the highest caliber of whitetail deer hunting in the country. At the deer lodge, it is their desire to make your stay one that you will not forget. Food is prepared by great cooks and served hot and fresh. When you hunt Enon, you will experience southern hospitality at its finest.

Enon Wingshooting

This is true plantation style bobwhite quail hunting at its finest. Intense game management of over 10,000 acres of land has insured over the years and today that Enon is indeed an exceptional quail hunting experience.

Old fashioned horseback quail hunting with a mule-drawn wagon suits some guests. Others enjoy jeep hunts. Both are readily available. In addition to its fine wild quail hunting, Enon also offers liberated bird hunts for those who prefer it.

Quality, well-trained pointing dogs and knowledgeable guides lead you to each covey across Enon's wide expanse of brush and wood. Visit the Enon Bird Dog Hall of Fame!

The excitement of a covey rise, of hunting with good friend, and of hunting with a brace of exceptional dogs adds up to the unmistakable feeling. The Enon spirit is something one may savor forever.

Deer Hunting

Enon Plantation offers the highest caliber whitetail deer hunting. Because it has a long heritage of management for quail hunting, Enon has had very little deer hunting over the years; furthermore, the quail management program provides an ideal habitat for deer. High quality feed patches are planted over the entire plantation containing corn, milo, clover, wheat, oats, and rye. Hardwoods have been left standing to provide cover, and fall plantings are made to enhance the trophy program for whitetails. Since the deployment of their deer management plan in 1993, the size of deer taken, number of large bucks taken, and number of large bucks seen by hunters has increased each season.

Enon's deer facility boasts a plethora of covered tower stands and easy-access lader stands in several prime locations across the plantation. Enon has its own modern processing facility. Their staff will handle everything for you when you arrive from your hunt, including skinning and dressing the deer, quartering and packing the meat, and putting your fresh venison in coolers for your trip home.

Deer Lodge Enon Plantation truly exemplifies southern hospitality. Each bedroom has its own bath and fireplace. There are also two guest cottages tastefully and comfortably decorated and have easy access to the Big House.

True Southern Dining and Hospitality

Enon Plantation

Rt. 2, Box 274
Midway, AL 36053

334-529-3325

Website: www.enon.com

Enon Plantation is located 140 miles from Atlanta by car and approximately 75 miles from Montgomery. To get to Enon, take the Opelika & Hurtsboro/Highway 51 exit (exit 60) off of Interstate 85.

Delicious home-cooked meals are prepared and served by Enon's courteous household staff. Enon boasts southern cooking that rivals even grandma's best.

ENON PLANTATION

Southern Fried Chicken

2   chickens, cut in pieces
2   tablespoons salt
3   cups flour
2   tablespoons pepper

- Salt chicken and set aside.
- Mix flour and pepper. Dredge chicken in flour mixture and let sit 30 minutes.
- Fry in deep iron skillet using very hot grease. Serves 8.

ENON PLANTATION

ENON PLANTATION

Chicken Pot Pie

1 chicken, cooked and deboned
1 can cream of chicken soup
½ soup can water
½ cup self-rising flour
1½ cups buttermilk
½ cup margarine, melted
2 cups chicken broth

- Place chicken meat in bottom of a greased 9 x 13-inch baking dish. Combine soup and water. Pour over chicken.

- Mix flour, buttermilk and margarine. Spread over chicken mixture. Spoon chicken broth over top.

- Bake in a preheated 350 degree oven 1 hour. Serves 6.

Baked Dove Breasts

¼ cup butter
1 cup white rice
8 dove breasts
½ package dry onion soup mix
1 can cream of mushroom or chicken soup

- Melt butter in a baking dish. Add rice and 1 cup water. Place dove breasts on rice. Sprinkle with dry soup mix.

- Combine canned soup and 1 cup water. Pour over dove. Bake in a preheated 350 degree oven for 1 hour. Serves 4.

Salmon Patties

2 eggs, lightly beaten
1 (15-ounce) can pink salmon, rinsed and drained
⅓ cup chopped onion
¼ cup flour
¼ cup cornmeal
5 crackers, crushed
pepper

- Combine eggs, salmon and onion.

- Mix flour, cornmeal, cracker crumbs and pepper. Add to salmon mixture. Form into patties and fry until golden brown. Serves 4.

ENON PLANTATION

Bread Pudding

4	hot dog or hamburger buns
8	eggs
3	cups sugar
4	cups milk
2	tablespoons vanilla
1	cup margarine, melted

- Preheat oven to 400 degrees.
- Place buns in a buttered 9 x 13-inch baking dish. Combine eggs and sugar, blending well. Add milk, vanilla and margarine. Pour over buns.
- Bake 30 minutes. Serves 8.

Peach Cobbler

½	cup butter or margarine
1	cup sugar
1	cup evaporated milk
¾	cup self-rising flour
1	large can peaches

- Melt butter in a baking dish. Mix sugar, milk and flour in a medium bowl. Add butter. Stir in peaches and blend well. Return to baking dish.
- Bake in preheated 350 degree oven until brown, about 45 minutes. Serves 8.

ENON PLANTATION

Chocolate Chip Cake

- 1 box yellow cake mix
- 1 small package instant vanilla pudding
- 1 cup vegetable oil
- 4 eggs
- 1 cup milk
- 1 bar German sweet chocolate, grated
- 1 cup chopped pecans
- ½ package semisweet chocolate morsels

Glaze:
- ½ cup butter
- 3 tablespoons cocoa
- 5 tablespoons evaporated milk
- 1 box powdered sugar, sifted
- 1 teaspoon vanilla
- 1 cup chopped nuts

- Combine cake mix, pudding, oil, eggs and milk in a large mixing bowl. Mix for 5 minutes. Stir in chocolate, nuts and morsels.

- Transfer to a greased and floured tube or Bundt pan. Bake in a preheated 325 degree oven for 55 minutes. Cover with foil and bake 15 minutes more.

- For Glaze: Place butter, cocoa and milk in a medium saucepan. Bring to a boil and remove from heat. Add sugar gradually, beating until smooth. Stir in vanilla and nuts. Pour over hot cake.

Southern Pecan Pie

- 2 cups chopped pecans
- 1 unbaked 9-inch deep-dish pie crust or 2 9-inch pie crusts
- 2 tablespoons butter or margarine, melted
- 3 eggs, beaten
- 1 cup sugar
- 1 cup dark corn syrup
- 1 teaspoon vanilla
- pinch of salt

- Pour pecans into bottom of pie crust.

- Combine butter, eggs, sugar, syrup, vanilla and salt. Pour over pecans.

- Bake in a preheated 325 degree oven for 1 hour.

Twilight casts a welcoming glow on the restaurant at Henderson Village

Henderson Village

Henderson Village reflects the past while looking to the future. Bernard Schneider was only nine years old when, in his native Germany, he saw American movies that portrayed grand Southern landscapes. He knew that someday he had to see those romantic images for himself, and he found them in central Georgia.

Schneider, an electronics entrepreneur, came to the United States in the 1960s on business with the intention of buying land near Atlanta because of the direct flights to and from Munich. That initial purchase has blossomed into 8,500 acres and includes pecan groves, cotton and peanut fields, ponds, and gamelands that are a part of ABS Farms, as well as the property now known as Henderson Village.

The concept behind Henderson Village was to preserve Southern vernacular architecture and lifestyle to create the same kind of Southern community that prospered during the cotton era. As a result, in July of 1998, Henderson Village opened its doors. A collection of 19th-century homes and cottages, it's located at what was once a thriving stagecoach stop at the intersection of Georgia Highway 26 and U.S. Highway 41. The century-old homes—some original to the property and others that have been moved there—indeed recall the beauty and romance of the "Old South." Dollie Newberry, 95, from nearby Perry, describes the village as "glorious." Not that she isn't just a bit partial to the place. Her great-grandfather, E. T. McGehee, built Langston House (which now serves as the restaurant) in 1838. Dollie herself lived for 77 years in the Newberry House (circa 1906), which she sold to Schneider in 1995. The Newberry House, at present, is home to Stuart MacPherson, the general manager of Henderson Village.

However, neither the staff nor Schneider himself are content to rest on their laurels. Plans call for the current 24 rooms to be increased; another 8 to 10 cottages will house 5 or 6 suites each. (Each room, including the ones already in place, will have a historical account of those who lived and worked there.) In addition, various craft shops are on the drawing board, set to feature quilts, pottery, furniture, and other decorative arts native to the area. The blacksmith's barn on the property will be opened for demonstrations and, for the athletically inclined, there will be tennis courts and a jogging path.

To make Henderson Village a true pampering experience, the property plans to feature all the makings of a European-style spa. Offering a cleansing of the mind and the spirit, the facility will include everything from motivational classes to nutritional advice and aromatherapy massages to therapeutic dips in different kinds of waters.

The best of the past is looking to the future. And the future, indeed, looks bright.

For more information about Henderson Village or to make reservations, consumers should call 1-888-615-9722 or visit their Internet site at www.hendersonvillage.com.

A Wealth of Experiences Await Henderson Village Guests

It's more than a relaxing retreat, it's a getaway where guests are tempted to wile away the hours rocking on their own private porches. At Henderson Village, there's seemingly no end to the ways visitors can spend their spare time.

Those who like to explore can leisurely stroll the grounds' 18 acres and discover the property's many offerings, as well as its many occupants. (They'll more than likely be joined by Angus, the general manager's golden retriever/Australian shepherd mix—and the unofficial "mascot.") In the heart of Henderson Village, there's a grand aviary that's home to 20 exotic birds. And, just a few steps further is an affiable menagerie that includes horses, donkeys, ostriches, chickens, South African Watusi cattle, and a pigmy goat, Billy.

Want to go further afield? Henderson Village's staff can direct guests to one of the newly blazed walking trails and provide guided mountain bike rides. Or, for those who prefer a little "horsepower," eight horses await riders for guided trail rides. The equine population of Henderson Village pulls its weight in other ways, too. Horse-drawn carriage rides are available for $15 each (free to Sunday brunch guests) and, in the near future, Fred and Wilma (a pair of resident mules) will offer hay rides.

Henderson Village is owned by Bernard Schneider, who generously shares his surrounding property—which includes lakes, woods and gamelands—with his guests. Nine ponds are stocked for fishing, and fly fishing instruction is available. There also are opportunities for turkey, deer, and wild boar hunting, as well as quail hunting on horseback. For those who prefer to practice their precision shooting on clay pigeons, there's a shooting range with its own secluded lodge.

Some guests may feel it's not a real vacation unless they have the chance to play golf. Golf-aholics can play two courses in the vicinity. The Southern Hills Golf Club in nearby Hawkinsville, located on the Ocmulgee River, is a new course that offers six miles of cart paths. In Perry, the well-established Houston Lake Country Club has been ranked among Georgia's top 50 courses by Golf Week Magazine.

At the end of the day, back at Henderson Village, guests can take a refreshing dip in the pool, relax in the chaise lounges surrounding the pool or in one of the twin gazebos that offer dappled shade and cool breezes. For the ultimate relaxation, guests can schedule an in-room massage.

After a full day of tailor-made experiences, it's time to think about a gourmet dinner at the property's Langston House Restaurant…as well as new experiences to come tomorrow.

The new general manager of Henderson Village is a long way from his homeland, but with his outgoing and friendly approach to people, he still seems right at home in south Houston County.

A native of Inverness, Scotland (famed as the home of the legendary Loch Ness monster), Stuart Macpherson came to this country seven years ago to work at Blantyre, an inn in Lenox, Massachusetts.

Since that time he has worked in management at Keswick Hall, Charlottesville, Virginia, and the Main Street Inn at Hilton Head Island, South Carolina.

Now, at 31, with his wife Susannah soon to join him here, Macpherson is succeeding David Dew as general manager of Henderson Village.

Macpherson has big plans for Henderson Village, an elegant, restored "country retreat" which offers gourmet dining at the Langston House Restaurant.

Henderson Village has gotten regional attention and will soon be featured in the magazine "Southern Living," but Macpherson is also interested in building business in the surrounding communities.

With the goal of attracting more business from Perry, Macon County and Dooly County, Macpherson is working on a neighbor's rate program. He has already established a moderately priced daily lunch menu.

"We're extending a hand to the community," he said, "and asking for support."

Gamelands Info

Whitetail Deer

Henderson Village Gamelands consists of 10,000 acres located in the heart of trophy buck country, incorporating land in Dooly, Houston, and Macon counties. Two of these counties, Dooly and Macon, are famous for producing Boone and Crockett Bucks. They are also under the Quality Deer Management Program for the State of Georgia. Working closely with the Georgia State Game and Fish Division, Henderson Village Gamelands is under intense quality game and land management.

Quail Hunting

Quail hunting is an old Southern tradition passed down to each generation. They offer liberated, as well as wild birds, for that avid wing shooter accompanied by some of the finest bird dogs in the country.

Fishing

Henderson Village Gamelands offers eight fishing ponds, stocked with bream, bass, catfish, and crappie. They also offer river and lake trips. Fishing may be combined with wild boar and turkey hunt packages.

Wild Boar

Big Creek runs through the plantation creating an abundant Feral and Russian hog population. Boars frequently top the scales at 500 pounds and make a nice addition to anyone's trophy room. Wild boar hunting is offered year-round.

The Gamelands Dove Hunts

Morning and Afternoon Hunts
10 people minimum
Includes:
• Bar-B-Que prior to hunt
• Soft Drinks served in the field
• Dinner at The Langston House
• Luxurious accommodation at the Inn

Quail Hunts

by mule team and horseback
Full day hunts for 4 people includes:
• One game of five stand
• Evening meal at The Langston House
• Overnight accommodations
• Breakfast at The Langston House
• Morning Hunt
• Field lunch

Trophy Deer Hunts

Three Day Trophy Combo Hunt (Rifle Only)
(Rut Only—November 1st–November 30th)
You may harvest 1 trophy buck (16-inch outside spread)
1 male hog (100 pounds or more)
Three Day Trophy Combo Hunt (Rifle Only)
You may harvest 1 trophy buck (16-inch outside spread)
1 male hog (100 pounds or more)

See Chip Shelton, Gamelands Manager, for more information on these exciting hunts.

Five Stand Sporting Clays is Now Open!

"For skeet-shooting enthusiasts," Macpherson said, "Henderson Village has opened a National Sporting Clay Association (NSCA) Sporting Clay Five Stand which will be open to the public."

Night Time Shoots Also Available up to 9:30 p.m.

*For information on these services,
call Stuart Macpherson at 912-988-8696.*

For more information about Henderson Village or to make reservations, consumers should call 1-888-615-9722 or visit their web site at www.hendersonvillage.com.

Fine Dining at Henderson Village Is a Worldly Experience

As Executive Chef at Henderson Village, Garry Kenley may be a long way from his native Scotland, but his culinary style is right at home. Combining his past experiences with his present locale, Kenley's creations are, as he describes, "Southern with a European twist."

Kenley grew up appreciating fine dining; his father was a chef and Kenley has enjoyed cooking since he was 15 years old. His formal training in the United Kingdom was classical French and he's spent time in numerous places throughout the world, developing an appreciation for different cultures and Epicurean delights.

Since Kenley's arrival at Henderson Village's Langston House Restaurant, he draws on his "fertile imagination" as he incorporates his worldly culinary education into the menu's tantalizing entrees and desserts. Some of his signature dishes include hot and sour seared yellow-fin tuna with a bacon, asparagus, and new potato salad and green pesto; roast rack of lamb with a blue-corn-chip-and-basil crust that is complimented with Mongolian fire pot sausage, couscous, and a smoked cheddar and horseradish sauce; white pepper ice cream with Scottish shortbread biscuits; deep-fried brown bread ice cream with coconut molasses sauce, and a warm fried green tomato tart with Chinese five-spice ice cream.

The one constant is that each of Kenley's creations incorporate local produce. Whether it's green peas or yellow squash, blueberries or peaches, he finds a way to use them in his frequently changing menus. Herbs plays an important role in Henderson Village's cuisine, evidenced by the beautiful herb garden outside the kitchen's back patio. "I don't follow trends," says Kenley, "I simply start with the best ingredients. I may be influenced by Japanese, Chinese, Thai, European and American cuisines, but my cooking is about using produces from the area."

For more information about Henderson Village's Langston House Restaurant, Executive Chef Garry Kenley, or to make reservations, consumers should call the property at 888-615-9722 or visit their Internet site at www.hendersonvillage.com.

The restaurant also offers a country brunch on Sundays with a free carriage ride around the village grounds, and has just introduced a spa with massage therapy.

HENDERSON VILLAGE

Roast Rack of Lamb with Blue Corn Chip and Basil Crust, Mongolian Fire Pot Sausage, Couscous and a Smoked Cheddar and Horseradish Sauce

8 racks New Zealand lamb
1 small package fried blue corn chips, ground
1 small bunch basil, chopped
6 tablespoons olive oil
1 tablespoon bread crumbs
2 cloves garlic, finely chopped

Sausage:
1 pound minced lean pork
¼ pound minced bacon
¼ pound minced pork fat
2 tablespoons hoisin sauce
2 tablespoons harissa
1 small bunch cilantro, chopped
sausage skins

Couscous:
8 ounces couscous
1½ cups hot water
4 tablespoons lemon juice
salt
cumin
chopped cilantro

Sauce:
1 cup white wine
2 cups lamb stock
2 tablespoons horseradish
2 cloves garlic, chopped
4 ounces smoked cheddar cheese, shredded
1 cup whipping cream

- Fry lamb rack on both sides for a few minutes to seal flavor.

- Combine corn chips, basil, olive oil, bread crumbs and garlic. Spread over tops of racks.

- Bake in a preheated 375 degree oven for 8 minutes.

- For Sausage: Combine all ingredients. Push into sausage skins, sealing both ends with a twist. Grill 4 minutes on each side.

- For Couscous: Place couscous, water and lemon juice in a saucepan. Season to taste with salt, cumin and cilantro. Steam until done.

- For Sauce: Reduce white wine by half over medium heat. Add stock, horseradish and garlic. Cook for 10 minutes. Stir in cheese and cream and cook over low heat, stirring, until cheese melts.

- To Assemble: Put couscous a plate and top with sliced sausage and lamb rack. Drizzle with sauce. Serves 8.

HENDERSON VILLAGE

Hot and Sour Seared Yellowfin Tuna with a Bacon Asparagus and New Potato Salad and Green Pesto

- 2 tablespoons rice wine vinegar
- 2 tablespoons sugar
- 1 teaspoon soy sauce
- 1 chili pepper, finely diced
- 1 tablespoon sesame oil
- 1 small piece fresh ginger, finely chopped
- 8 (6-ounce) pieces tuna
- ½ pound hickory bacon, finely chopped
- 1 pound asparagus, roughly chopped
- 1 pound new potatoes, cooked and cubed
- 1 Vidalia onion, finely chopped
- 1 teaspoon horseradish sauce

Pesto:
- 1 large bunch basil
- 2 tablespoons pine nuts
- 10 tablespoons olive oil
- 4 cloves garlic
- 2 ounces grated Parmesan cheese
- 2 tablespoons white wine

- Combine vinegar, sugar, soy sauce, chili pepper, sesame oil and ginger in a small saucepan. Bring to a boil, reduce heat and simmer 5 minutes. Remove from heat and chill.

- Place tuna in a shallow dish, cover with chilled dressing and marinate 2 hours.

- Lightly oil a wok and heat until very hot. Fry bacon and onion for a few minutes. Add asparagus and cook for a few minutes. Turn off heat, add potatoes and horseradish and mix lightly. Season to taste.

- For Pesto: Combine all ingredients in a food processor and process until smooth.

- Grill tuna to your liking.

- To serve, place asparagus salad in a large bowl. Top with tuna and drizzle with pesto.

HENDERSON VILLAGE

Cappicola Ham, Boursin Cheese and Leek Crêpe

Crêpe Batter:
- 2 eggs
- 1 cup milk
- 6 ounces all-purpose flour, sifted
- 2 tablespoons vegetable oil
- pinch of salt

Filling:
- ¼ cup butter
- 2 large leeks, thinly sliced
- 2 cloves garlic, finely chopped
- 1 (8-ounce) package Boursin cheese
- 2 ounces Monterey Jack cheese, shredded
- 8 ounces thinly sliced cappicola ham

Sauce:
- 2 cups vegetable stock
- 1 clove garlic, minced
- 1 onion, chopped
- 1 cup whipping cream
- 2 tablespoons Dijon mustard

- For Crêpes: Mix eggs, salt, milk and oil. Stir in flour to make a thin batter. Heat a crêpe pan very hot. Pour a thin layer of batter over base of pan. Cook one minute. Flip crêpe and cook for another minute. Remove from pan and continue, making 8 crêpes in all.

- For Filling: Melt butter on medium heat. Sauté leeks and garlic until slightly soft. Drain in a colander. While still hot, mix in the cheeses.

- Divide mixture among crêpes and spread evenly. Top each crêpe with 2 slices ham. Roll up and place on a baking sheet. Bake in preheated 350 degree oven for 5 minutes.

- For Sauce: Reduce vegetable stock by half over medium heat. Add garlic and onion. Cook for 5 more minutes. Stir in cream and mustard and cook, stirring, until smooth and hot.

Serves 6 to 8.

HENDERSON VILLAGE

Warm Fried Green Tomato Tart with Chinese Five Spice Ice Cream

Pastry:
2   cups all-purpose flour
½   cup powdered sugar
¾   cup butter, cubed and chilled
2   eggs, beaten
pinch of salt

Ice Cream:
6   egg yolks
½   cup sugar, divided
2¼   cups milk
2   teaspoons Chinese five spice powder
1   vanilla bean, split
½   cup whipping cream

Filling:
3   green tomatoes, sliced
butter
½   cup plus 1 tablespoon sugar, divided
2   eggs, beaten
1   cup whipping cream
¼   cup ground almonds

- For Pastry: Lightly blend flour, salt, sugar and butter to a crumb. Add eggs slowly. Lightly mix for 1 minute. Cover and chill for 1 hour. Roll out pastry and place in a pie plate. Prick with a fork and bake in a preheated 350 degree oven for 5 minutes.

- For Ice Cream: Beat egg yolks and ¼ cup sugar in a bowl until light and fluffy. Place milk, remaining sugar, five spice powder and vanilla bean in a saucepan. Bring to a boil. Remove from heat and slowly whisk into egg mixture. Mix well. Return to pan and cook over low heat, stirring constantly, until mixture coats spoon. Do not boil. Remove from heat and pass through a sieve. Chill.

- Churn chilled custard and cream in an ice cream machine for 20 minutes or until ready.

- For Filling: Lightly fry tomatoes in a small amount of butter and 1 tablespoon sugar until golden, 2 to 3 minutes.

- Place over pie crust. Beat eggs, remaining sugar and cream until well blended. Pour over tomatoes. Sprinkle with almonds. Bake in a preheated 350 degree oven until custard is set. Serve warm with ice cream.

HENDERSON VILLAGE

HENDERSON VILLAGE

Brownie Honey and Maple Syrup Cheesecake with Peanut Brittle Sauce

1	cup graham crackers, ground
1	cup powdered sugar, divided
½	cup melted butter
1	pound cream cheese, softened
2	tablespoons honey, warmed
2	tablespoons maple syrup
1	small package brownies, crushed
1	cup whipping cream
6	leaves gelatin
¼	cup cold water

Peanut Brittle Sauce:

1	tablespoon molasses
2	tablespoons hazelnut liqueur
¼	cup whipping cream
¼	cup peanut brittle, finely ground
8	ounces natural yogurt

- Line bottom and sides of an 8-inch spring form pan with baking parchment. Combine graham cracker crumbs, ½ cup powdered sugar and butter. Press into bottom of pan and chill.

- Place cream cheese, honey, remaining ½ cup powdered sugar and brownies in a blender. Process for 1 minute. Add cream and mix 1 more minute.

- Put gelatin and water in a pan over low heat. Melt and add to cheese mixture when liquefied. Blend for 30 minutes.

- Pour into prepared crust and chill for 3 hours.

- For Sauce: Combine molasses and liqueur in a saucepan. Cook over low heat for a few minutes. Add cream and peanut brittle and cook for 5 minutes. Remove from heat and stir in yogurt. Serve over cheesecake.

Mansfield Plantation

Once upon a time, Georgetown County was the major rice producing area in the United States. Rice Plantations lined the banks of the Black, Pee Dee, and Waccamaw Rivers from Georgetown City to the county line.

Mansfield Plantation is the only plantation on the west bank of the Black River in Georgetown County that survives today essentially as it was when rice was grown here in the mid-19th century.

Mansfield Plantation began with a land grant to John Green in 1718. For the next 128 years, Mansfield was operated by absentee landowners. In 1846, Mansfield was acquired by Dr. Francis S. Parker from his father-in-law, the Reverend Maurice H. Lance. Dr. Parker, a physician and rice planter from Charleston and Goose Creek, made Mansfield his principle winter residence.

Dr. Parker rapidly expanded his rice planting operation, acquiring Greenwich Plantation and later the adjacent Willowbank Plantation which were located in what is now Georgetown City. As a result of these efforts and expansions, Dr. Parker's rice crop increased from 375,000 pounds in 1850 to 1,440,000 pounds in 1860. During the same period of time the compensation paid to overseers for the daily management of the plantations increased from $300 per year to $1,600 per year, and the number of slaves on the three plantations increased from one hundred twenty-eight to two hundred thirty-five. (see manuscript plantation journals for Mansfield Plantation and Greenwich and Willowbank Plantations, South Carolinian Library, University of South Carolina, Columbia, S.C.)

Dr. Parker was also involved in local politics. He served as Commissioner of Free Schools for Georgetown County, attended the South Carolina Secession Convention, where he signed the Ordinance of Secession, and served as Provost Marshall of Georgetown County during the War for Southern Independence.

Mansfield Plantation retains the original romantic mystique of the Old South, as well as much of its original architecture. The main house was originally built in 1812, expanded by Dr. Parker, and embellished by Colonel Robert Montgomery during his ownership from 1930 to 1970. Local lore that the house at Mansfield was burned by Federal troops at the end of the War are false. One of Dr. Parker's houses was burned, but it was the house at Greenwich Plantation, not Mansfield. (see, for instance, George C. Rogers, THE HISTORY OF GEORGETOWN COUNTY, SOUTH CAROLINA, p. 1461.)

The Mansfield slave village contains five original antebellum slave cabins, as well as two replicas built in the 1930's, and an antebellum slave chapel. The original winnowing house, used to separate the chaff from the rice seed, survives today.

Duck Hunting at Mansfield

Mansfield, in a nutshell, consists of 900 acres of pure South Carolina low country with the crowning jewels (to the duck hunter) being 2 rice ponds of 35 to 50 acres. Wildlife abounds with the most being "deer and gators." Surrounded by dikes that allow for seasonal draining and planting, the ponds are home to eight floating blinds and numerous stock blinds on the dikes themselves. This setup helps to position gunners along any observed flight.

Come and enjoy hunting mallards, wood ducks, teel, and pintails in Mansfield marshes and old rice fields. Also Mansfield allows dogs, says the Innkeeper, who adds proudly "We have a four-paw rating."

Mansfield may not be for every duck hunter out there, but for those who want to experience superior low country gunning in a unique atmosphere, it is just the ticket.

Lodging

The natural beauty of Mansfield with its massive lawns and moss-veiled oaks, makes it an ideal spot for relaxing or entertaining. The Black River is perfect for kayaking and canoeing. Expeditions can be arranged for canoe and kayak renting as well as guided tours with a naturalist.

Dining

The main plantation house features high ceilings, elaborate wood work, and heart of pine floors. The house is filled with period antiques which include furniture, French porcelain, gilt chandeliers and candlesticks, large gilt framed mirrors, and American paintings, both portraits and landscapes.

MANSFIELD PLANTATION

Old Fashioned Pig Roast with BBQ Sauce

1   90 pound pig
vinegar
salt

BBQ Sauce:

1   gallon vinegar
½   cup sugar
¼   cup salt
juice of 3 lemons
3   tablespoons cayenne pepper
3   tablespoons pepper
1   cup butter
1½   cups firmly packed brown sugar
1   small bottle smoke flavoring
1   large onion, chopped
1   (8-ounce) bottle ketchup
3   tablespoons mustard

- Cut off head and feet of pig. Split down center of the stomach side. Lay pig flat, stomach-side-down, over grill. Rub back well with vinegar and salt. Cook for 11 hours.

- Turn pig on its back and make slits all over. Pour the sauce into slits. Cook for 3 hours more, basting with sauce every 30 minutes.

- For Sauce: Combine all ingredients and bring to a boil. Simmer 10 minutes. Strain and brush on pig last 3 hours of cooking.

MANSFIELD PLANTATION

Mom's Shrimp Creole

4	tablespoons butter
4	tablespoons flour
1	cup chopped green onions
½	cup chopped celery
½	cup chopped green bell pepper
2	tablespoons chopped parsley
1	clove garlic, crushed
1	(8-ounce) can Spanish-style tomato sauce
1	(16-ounce) can whole tomatoes
1½	cups hot water
1½	teaspoons salt
⅛	teaspoon cayenne pepper
¼	teaspoon hot pepper sauce
¼	teaspoon thyme
1	bay leaf
½	teaspoon sugar
1½	pounds peeled, deveined shrimp

- Melt butter. Add flour to make a roux. Add onions, celery, bell pepper, parsley and garlic. Cook for 5 minutes, stirring so that vegetables do not brown. Add remaining ingredients except shrimp. Bring to a boil, reduce heat, cover and simmer 30 minutes. Just before serving, return to a boil, add shrimp and bring to another boil. Remove from heat and serve over rice.

MANSFIELD PLANTATION

Grandmother's Gingerbread

½ cup butter, softened
½ cup firmly packed brown sugar
2 tablespoons mild molasses
1 cup warm milk
3 cups all-purpose flour
⅓ cup ground ginger
5 tablespoons instant coffee granules
¾ teaspoon salt
½ teaspoon cinnamon
½ teaspoon mace
½ teaspoon nutmeg
3 eggs, beaten
juice and grated rind of 1 large orange
1 teaspoon baking soda dissolved in 2 tablespoons warm water

- Combine butter and brown sugar in a mixing bowl and beat until smooth. Add molasses and milk and blend well.

- Sift together flour, salt, ginger, cinnamon, mace and nutmeg. Add to batter with eggs, orange juice and rind. Mix until well blended. Add baking soda mixture last. Pour into a greased and floured loaf pan.

- Bake in a preheated 350 degree oven until a tester inserted in center comes out clean, about 45 minutes to one hour.

Dad's Fruit Cobbler

¼ cup butter
1 cup sugar
1 cup all-purpose flour
1½ teaspoons baking powder
⅔ cup milk
½ teaspoon curry powder
1 can fruit or 2½ cups fresh fruit plus ⅔ cup sugar

- Melt butter in a deep-dish casserole.

- Stir together sugar, flour, baking powder, milk and curry in a medium bowl. Pour over melted butter.

- Add fruit. Shake mixture down and cover. Bake in a preheated 350 degree oven for 1 hour.

Mansfield Plantation Bed and Breakfast Country Inn

1776 Mansfield Road
Georgetown, SC 29440

843-546-6961
843-546-5235 (Fax)
800-355-3223
www.bbonline.com/sc/mansfield/ (website)

Sally and Jim Cahalan, Proprietors

Tours are available by advance appointment with 12 or more.

Pinewood Plantation

Pinewood Plantation is nestled among 1,900 acres of longleaf pine and wiregrass pineland. Located only 20 miles south of Albany, Pinewood will give you the opportunity to hunt and fish southern style on one of the finest plantations in South Georgia. The lodge has been totally remodeled and furnished to provide a relaxed and comfortable atmosphere that will accommodate up to 18 people.

Pinewood has many wild bobwhite quail coveys and white tail deer (viewing only) waiting for you. Our bobwhite quail population is increased by controlled releasing at regular intervals.

Hunting at Pinewood

Once you have visited the habited and hunting courses, you will soon know why South Georgia still claims the title of Quail Capital of the World. Maintaining the wild quail habitat in addition to bird hunting, Pinewood is concerned about quail conservation as well as providing excellent shooting opportunities for hunters of all levels.

Travel the grounds aboard wagons pulled behind jeeps with superior quality, well-trained dogs. If you like, a trap range for sharpening your shooting skills is available before taking on the quail.

Dining

Enjoy traditional Southern style meals prepared by Pinewood's fine staff. Some say it's the best country cooking in the South!

With bunkhouse style, single and double accommodations, the lodge is complete with recreation room, conference room and dining room.

PINEWOOD PLANTATION

Chicken Breast in Wine and Mushroom Sauce

- 1 boneless, skinless chicken breast per person
- ¼ cup margarine
- 3 tablespoons flour
- 2 cups milk
- ½ cup cooking sherry
- 1 large can mushrooms, drained

- Dredge chicken in flour and fry until half done. Place in a casserole dish which has been coated with nonstick spray.

- Melt margarine in a heavy saucepan. Blend in flour. Add milk and stir until it begins to thicken. Do not allow it to get too thick. Add sherry and mushrooms. Cook 5 minutes longer.

- Pour over chicken, cover with foil and bake in a preheated 350 degree oven for 45 minutes. Serve over rice pilaf.

PINEWOOD PLANTATION

Fried Quail

2 quails per person
3 eggs per every 5 birds
garlic salt
seasoning salt
pepper
paprika
flour

- Wash and clean quail. Pick off any feathers that may be left on bird. Drain water off birds and place in a large container.

- Break eggs directly on birds. Sprinkle with garlic salt, seasoning salt, pepper and paprika to taste. Toss eggs and seasonings over birds with hands until a nice marinade develops. Refrigerate for 2 hours, tossing birds in marinade at least twice.

- Put flour in a large bowl. Shake excess marinade from birds, roll in flour. Heat cooking oil in a deep fryer to 350 degrees. Fry birds for about 8 minutes, depending on size. Drain on paper towels.

PINEWOOD PLANTATION

Stuffed and Wrapped Chicken Breasts

1 boneless chicken breast per person
1 slice honey-baked ham per person
swiss cheese
sliced bacon
1 can cream of chicken soup
parsley

- Trim all fat and skin from chicken. Place skin-side down on cutting board. Flatten with a meat mallet.

- Place a slice of ham and cheese on each breast and roll up. Wrap bacon around each breast and secure with a toothpick. Place in a casserole dish which has been coated with nonstick spray.

- Spoon soup over breasts and sprinkle with parsley. Cover with foil and bake in a preheated 350 degree oven for 45 minutes. Remove foil and bake 30 minutes more. Serve over rice pilaf.

PINEWOOD PLANTATION

PINEWOOD PLANTATION

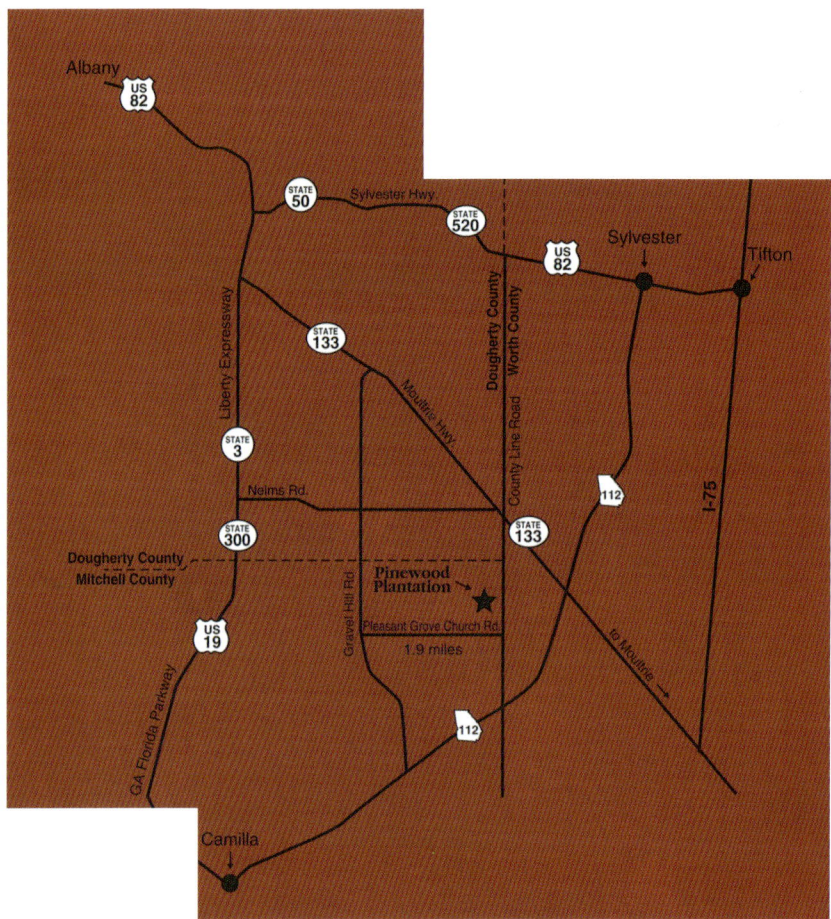

Pinewood Plantation

E-mail: pinewod@surfsouth.com
Phone: 912-483-0770

Pinway Plantation

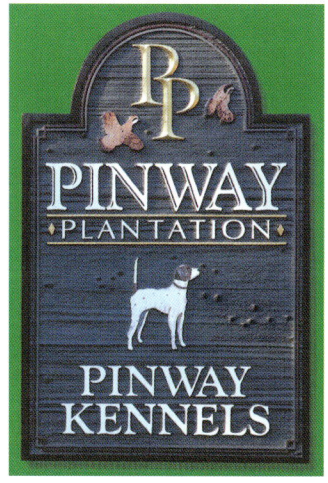

Pinway Plantation is located in the picturesque Jefferson and Burke Counties of Georgia just 30 miles south of Bush Field Airport and the city of Augusta.

From 1929 to 1951, Pinway was a working cotton plantation. In 1951, it was sold to the Mennonites who converted the crop to a variety of vegetables and supplied local markets. In 1979, Pinway was sold and was transformed into Quail Haven Farms, a successful quail farm operated for 19 years. In 1998, Pinway Plantation with all its grandeur became a hunting plantation. Pinway boasts 1,300 acres of planted pines, open fields and a 250 acre secluded duck pond. Pinway is one of the premier hunting plantations in the southeast due to a combination of acreage, lodging, pastures, timber, ponds, and wildlife habitats which act as natural breeding and feeding grounds for large coveys of quail, dove, duck, turkey, and herds of deer.

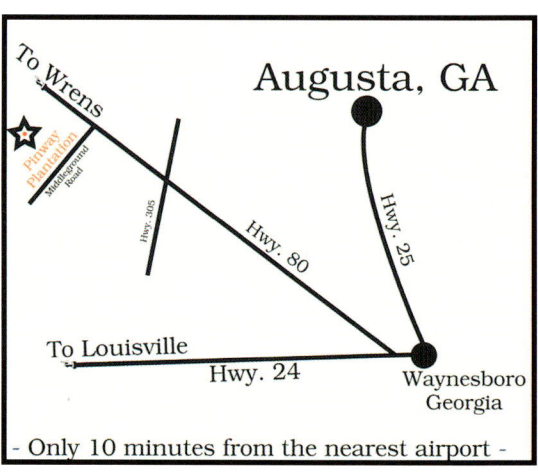

For more information and reservations, call:

Toll free: 1-877-634-2688
Tel.: 912-634-2688
Fax: 912-634-0117
16983 Middleground Rd.
Wrens, Georgia 30833

Contact us by e-mail for a free brochure!
Lsp@pinwayplantation.com

Hunting at Pinway

Pinway Plantation is located twelve miles west of Waynesboro, Georgia, the Bird Dog Capital of the World. Many have visited with us and experienced our quail, deer and turkey hunts. Earlier this year we purchased another 250 acres that includes a beautifully secluded duck pont. It won't be long before duck calls will be heard as the mist rises to greet the ducks. Klaus, our champion black lab, is ready to retrieve your many ducks.

Seasoned guides are on staff to enhance the hunt for the inexperienced as well as the experienced. 1,500 acres of planted pines and open field to offer the South's finest "Olde Plantation" quail, deer and turkey hunting with trained English pointers and setters.

Dining

Pinway's covered dock is a great place to gather for lunch and casual conversation. The gathering room in the lodge is always a favorite place for relaxing, or you can also play a game of pool in the billiard room.

Southern gourmet meals are a specialty at Pinway. They would like to share some of their favorites with you.

PINWAY PLANTATION

Southern Pimiento Cheese

12 ounces sharp cheddar cheese, grated
⅓ (16-ounce) jar smoke-flavored cheese spread
1½ cups mayonnaise
½ teaspoon pepper
dash of garlic
salt or garlic powder to taste
1 tablespoon juice drained from bottled peppers

- Combine all ingredients. Cover and refrigerate overnight.

Artichoke and Spinach Casserole

3 (10-ounce) packages frozen chopped spinach
4 teaspoons butter
salt and pepper
2 (6-ounce) jars marinated artichoke hearts, drained and marinade reserved
3 (8-ounce) packages cream cheese, softened
2 tablespoons milk
1 tablespoon garlic powder
½ cup chopped onion
¾ cup grated Parmesan cheese

- Cook spinach according to package directions. Drain. Add butter and salt to taste. Moisten with a little of the reserved marinade.

- Arrange artichokes and remaining marinade in the bottom of a greased 1½-quart glass baking dish. Top with spinach.

- Combine cream cheese, milk, garlic powder and onion. Beat until smooth. Spread over spinach. Season with pepper to taste. Sprinkle with Parmesan. Cover and refrigerate for 24 hours.

- Bake in a preheated 375 degree oven for 40 minutes. Serves 8.

PINWAY PLANTATION

Plantation Cheese Grits

3 cups water
1 cup milk
1 teaspoon salt
1 cup grits
¼ cup butter
6 ounces sharp cheddar cheese, grated
2 eggs, separated
garlic powder to taste
¼ teaspoon paprika
cracker or bread crumbs, optional

- Combine water, milk and salt in a large saucepan. Bring to a boil and gradually stir in grits. Add butter and cheese, reduce heat and cook until desired consistency, stirring occasionally.

- Whisk in egg yolks, garlic powder and paprika. Beat egg whites until stiff. Fold into grits mixture.

- Pour into a greased 9 x 12-inch casserole. Top with crumbs, if desired. Bake in a preheated 350 degree oven for 45 minutes. Serves 4.

Pinway Breakfast Casserole

2 pounds sausage
12 slices bread, cubed
2 cups grated sharp cheddar cheese
9 eggs
2 cups milk
1½ teaspoons dry mustard

- Brown sausage and drain well.

- Place half of bread cubes in bottom of a greased casserole dish. Cover with half of sausage and sprinkle with half of cheese. Repeat layering with remaining bread, sausage and cheese.

- Combine eggs, milk and mustard, blending well. Pour over casserole, cover and refrigerate overnight.

- Bake in a preheated 350 degree oven until a knife inserted in center comes out clean, 45 minutes to 1 hour. Cut into squares to serve. Serves 8.

PINWAY PLANTATION

Mooney's Sour Cream Cornbread

¾ cup yellow cornmeal
¾ cup all-purpose flour
1 teaspoon salt
3 teaspoons baking powder
1 cup sour cream
2 eggs, lightly beaten
½ cup vegetable oil
butter, softened

- Combine cornmeal, flour, salt and baking powder in a mixing bowl. Add sour cream, eggs and oil. Stir until well blended.

- Pour into a greased 9-inch square pan. Bake in a preheated 400 degree oven 25 to 30 minutes. Spread with butter while warm. Serves 6.

Almond Mandarin Orange Salad

½ head red leaf lettuce
1 cup sliced celery
2 green onions, chopped
1 tablespoon minced parsley
1 cup mandarin oranges, drained
1 cup slivered almonds, roasted and salted

Dressing:

½ teaspoon salt
dash of pepper
¼ teaspoon hot pepper sauce
2 tablespoons sugar
2 tablespoons tarragon vinegar
¼ cup vegetable oil

- Tear lettuce into bite-size pieces and place in a salad bowl. Add remaining salad ingredients. Toss lightly, cover and chill.

- For Dressing: combine all ingredients in a blender and purée until blended. When ready to serve, pour over salad and toss to coat. Serves 2.

PINWAY PLANTATION

Mary Alice's Layered Salad

1 large jar mayonnaise
3 tablespoons sugar
1 head Bibb lettuce
1 (10-ounce) package frozen peas, thawed
1 cup shredded cheddar cheese
1 jar bacon bits

- Combine mayonnaise and sugar in a bowl. Let stand while making salad.

- Tear lettuce into bite-size pieces. Layer lettuce and peas in a large salad bowl. Spread top with mayonnaise mixture. Sprinkle with cheese and bacon bits. Let stand 10 minutes before serving. Serves 6.

Dove Delicious

12 doves, split
6 slices bacon, halved
4 potatoes, peeled and quartered
1 carrot, cut in ½-inch rounds
1 onion, chopped
¼ cup diced green bell pepper
salt and pepper
seasoning salt
worcestershire sauce
butter

- Place 2 doves on a 12-inch square of foil. Repeat with remaining doves.

- Place a piece on bacon on each dove. Arrange potatoes, carrots, onion and bell pepper around doves. Season with salt, pepper and seasoning salt to taste. Sprinkle with Worcestershire sauce and top with butter.

- Fold foil to seal. Arrange on baking sheets and bake in a preheated 325 degree oven for 1½ hours. Serve immediately. Serves 6.

PINWAY PLANTATION

Plantation Quail Dinner in a Bag

8   quail
1   small onion, chopped
1   green bell pepper, chopped
1   celery stalk, chopped
3   large potatoes, chopped
2   small bags baby carrots
4   ears corn
1   teaspoon salt
¼   teaspoon pepper
1   cup water
½   cup cooking wine

- Clean quail thoroughly and place in a large foil baking bag. Add remaining ingredients. Close bag tightly and place in a baking pan.

- Bake in a preheated 450 degree oven until done, about 45 minutes. Serves 6.

Pinway Plantation Fried Quail

12   quail breasts
salt and pepper
flour
1   onion, chopped
water

- Wash quail and pat dry. Sprinkle with salt and pepper and dredge in flour. Fry in cooking oil until done. Remove and drain.

- Reserve 2 to 3 tablespoons of oil from frying quail and discard rest. Sauté onion in oil until tender. Sprinkle with flour, stirring constantly. When flour is browned, season with salt and pepper. Stir in water until desired consistency is reached. Return quail to skillet and cook until tender. Serves 6.

PINWAY PLANTATION

Duck and Wild Rice Casserole

4 ducks
salt and pepper
1 onion, quartered
1 stalk celery, quartered
1 apple, quartered
1 bay leaf
1 (10-ounce) package long grain and wild rice with seasonings
1 onion, chopped
½ cup mayonnaise
2 (10¾-ounce) cans cream of celery soup
½ cup water chestnuts

- Place ducks, salt and pepper, quartered onion, celery, apple and bay leaf in a large stock pot. Cover with water, bring to a boil, reduce heat, cover and simmer 6 to 8 hours.

- Remove duck from broth to cool. Reserve and strain 1¾ cups broth, saving the rest for other uses, if desired.

- Debone cooled duck and place meat in a large mixing bowl. Add reserved stock and all remaining ingredients. Mix lightly and turn into a greased 9 x 12-inch casserole.

- Cover and bake in a preheated 350 degree oven for 1 hour. Serves 6.

Apple-Cranberry Compote

3 cooking apples, peeled and quartered
1 (16-ounce) can whole cranberry sauce
⅓ cup honey
dash of salt
1-2 cinnamon sticks

- Slow Cooker Method: Place apples in a slow cooker. Combine remaining ingredients and pour over apples. Cover and cook on high until apples are tender, about 2½ hours, stirring after one hour.

- Conventional Stove Method: Place apples in a saucepan with ¼ cup water. Bring to a boil, cover, reduce heat and simmer until apples are tender, 10 to 15 minutes, adding more water if necessary. Stir in remaining ingredients, cover and cook gently 10 minutes longer. Serves 4.

PINWAY PLANTATION

Ruth's Sour Cream Pound Cake

1 cup butter, softened
3 cups sugar
1 cup sour cream
1 teaspoon vanilla
½ teaspoon lemon extract
½ teaspoon almond extract
3 cups cake flour
¼ teaspoon baking soda
¼ teaspoon baking powder
6 eggs
nutmeg

- Cream butter and sugar until light and fluffy. Add sour cream and mix well. Add flavorings.

- Sift flour, baking soda and baking powder together. Add by thirds to butter mixture alternating with 2 eggs each time. Blend well after each addition.

- Pour into a greased tube pan and sprinkle with nutmeg. Bake in a preheated 325 degree oven until a tester inserted in center comes out clean, about 1 hour and 15 minutes. Serves 8.

Amaretto Brownies

1 package brownie mix
½ cup vegetable oil
3 eggs
6 tablespoons amaretto

Filling:
¾ cup butter, softened
2 cups powdered sugar
3 tablespoons amaretto

Topping:
6 ounces semisweet chocolate
4 tablespoons butter

- Prepare brownie mix according to package directions, using oil and 3 eggs. Omit water.

- Turn into a 9 x 13-inch greased baking dish.

- Bake in a preheated 350 degree oven until done, about 25 to 30 minutes. Remove from oven and sprinkle with amaretto. Cool completely.

- For Filling: Combine all ingredients and beat until smooth. Spread over brownies and refrigerate at least 1 hour.

- For Topping: Place chocolate and butter in a small saucepan. Melt over low heat, stirring constantly. Spread over topping, cover and chill. Cut into squares to serve. Serves 12.

PINWAY PLANTATION

Park Avenue Squares

- 1 package butter cake mix
- ½ cup butter, softened
- 3 eggs
- 1 cup chopped nuts
- 1 (8-ounce) package cream cheese, softened
- 1 (16-ounce) package powdered sugar

- Combine cake mix, butter, 1 egg and chopped nuts in a medium bowl. Press into a greased 9 x 13-inch baking dish.

- Lightly beat remaining 2 eggs in a medium bowl. Add cream cheese and combine well. Gradually add powdered sugar, beating until smooth. Spread over cake mixture.

- Bake in a preheated 350 degree oven for 30 to 40 minutes. Cut into squares to serve. Serves 8.

Southern Pecan Pie

- 3 eggs, lightly beaten
- 1 cup sugar
- 1 cup white corn syrup
- ¼ cup butter, melted
- 1 cup pecans
- 1 teaspoon vanilla
- 1 unbaked pie crust

- Combine eggs and sugar and mix thoroughly. Add syrup, butter, pecans and vanilla and blend well. Pour into pie crust.

- Bake in a preheated 350 degree oven until a knife inserted in center comes out clean, 45 minutes to 1 hour. Serves 8

Quail Country

LODGE & CONFERENCE CENTER

QUAIL COUNTRY
LODGE & CONFERENCE CENTER

Quail Country, known earlier as Sowega Hunting Club, was founded in 1971, by Rev. Thomas H. Newberry, Sr., and consisted of about 360 acres of land. A native of Early County, Tommy and his wife Ann created a unique hunting facility that allowed people from all over the world to take part in the South's finest quail shooting. Quail Country became a family affair with Tommy and Ann's children Kay and Tom becoming heavily involved in running the business.

Guests have traveled from as far as South America, California, Canada and Israel to hunt, relax, and enjoy the atmosphere and surroundings. Quail Country has also had its share of prominent guests including former President Jimmy Carter, country music legend Jimmy Dickens, actor Patrick Duffy, singer Louise Mandrell, actor Sonny Shroyer, and many more. Most recently, L.L. Bean representatives enjoyed a two week stay while taking photos for their 1999 Fall Hunting catalog. (They also shot their 1998 Fall Hunting catalog here.)

Quail Country is a proud sponsor and official land owner for Quail Unlimited, which is a non-profit organization committed to the preservation of the crucial upland game bird habitat, vitally needed to sustain healthy bird populations.

In 1992, Kay and her husband, Paschal Brooks, obtained ownership of Quail Country. With Tom as the hunting & farm manager, they took Quail Country into the future by building a new lodge in 1996, and adding a significant amount of hunting land. The new facility is equipped with a conference room, conference annex, computer outlet, Internet, fax, gift shop, etc. The state-of-the-art lodge measures 11,500 square feet and is located on the bank of "spring fed" Mill Creek.

The conference annex at Quail Country is also located 'on-the-creekbank' and is equipped with a very large smoker, grill facilities, and fish cleaning and cooking facilities. It is a stand-alone building and can be utilized for group cookings, meetings, suppers, etc.

Beginning with a dream and 360 acres, Quail Country has now excelled to over 9,500 acres and is a successful reality. Paschal and Kay firmly believe in offering guests the qualities that have been a part of Quail Country for 26 years. Traditions such as; offering excellent quail shooting, the best "home cooking" this side of the Mississippi, and of course lots of "Southern Hospitality."

Thank you for allowing Quail Country to serve you.

Ya'll be sure to come back!

South's Finest Quail Hunting

Quail Country, the oldest South Georgia quail shooting preserve west of the Flint river, lies at the heart of the "Quail Capital of the World." Here the habitat is perfect for the bobwhite, prince of all

gamebirds. In this day of dwindling quail habitat, a year-round program of habitat improvement as well as the latest in wildlife management techniques are utilized to ensure a good quail population. Feed plots are planted annually near natural cover to retain and encourage growth and development of all types of wild game population. The esthetic value of their woodland and agricultural areas are equally as important as their wildlife population. Outdoorsmen (and their ladies) come from all over the nation to try their skills sighting in on the fast flying bobs and hens. Shooters come back again and again for some of the 'sportiest shotgunning' on the face of the earth. Few ever forget the beautiful dog work, perfect points, and exploding coveys that stir a man's soul.

Relax aboard one of Quail Country's specially equipped hunting vehicles as your guide and a brace of fine hunting dogs hunt the elusive bobwhite quail. Quail Country is <u>not</u> your regular everyday 'run-of-the-mill' shooting/hunting preserve. Quail Country is *wingshooters paradise*.

Over 9500 acres are now under Quail Country wildlife management. The heart of this area is their 1,000 acre quail preserve hunting heaven, with a season that runs from October 1 to March 31, with no set state game limit of quail. Georgia state law dictates game limits and hunting seasons on the remaining 8,500 acres of forest and field. Native quail hunting season runs from about Thanksgiving through February. All quail hunts are conducted with trained guides and dogs and specially equipped jeeps or from our custom designed 'hunting

buggy.' Quail Country's hunting courses have been designed to provide you with an event that you will enjoy and remember as a truly unique 'Southern Style' hunting experience.

Deer hunting is available during season and combination quail/deer hunts are available.

Turkey hunts (guided or non-guided) are available during season.

Dove shoots are scheduled on agricultural fields of milo, millet, peanuts, corn and special peas.

Continental Pheasant shoots are very exciting and can be enjoyed by a group as an additional experience during a quail outing or can be attended individually on a reservation basis.

Let Quail Country assist you and your group in arranging the most relaxing and exciting hunting experience possible!

Quail Country's skeet and sporting clays shooting area is available for your use and is located at the Lodge. This is a special place for you to "warm up" before a hunt, shoot competitively, or to just shoot for the fun of it! Shooting is available year-round.

Lodging

Your on-site overnight lodging will be enjoyed while you relax in Quail Country's all-new 11,500 square foot Lodge, located on the bank of "spring-fed" Mill Creek. Quail Country Lodge offers 14 single/double bedrooms with private baths, two lounges with fireplaces, spacious dining area, conference room for meetings, and a gift shop. For groups of 12 or more, the entire lodge is reserved for your group's enjoyment. Many choose to bring along non-shooting guests just to relax and enjoy the atmosphere and surroundings.

Wake up and enjoy freshly brewed coffee in the lounge and a variety of juices as your breakfast is prepared and served. Lunch is served in the dining room following your return and brief rest from the morning's activities. Appetizers and refreshments may be enjoyed upon your return from the afternoon hunt as you relax in one of the two lounges or over at the 'Cookhouse.' Those that are hunting just for the day will be served lunch.

Quail Country's facilities are also available off-season for corporate retreats, planning meetings, or other group activities.

The Cookhouse at Quail Country Lodge is also located 'on-the-creekbank' and is equipped with a very large smoker, grill facilities, and fish cleaning and cooking facilities. It is a stand-alone building and can be utilized for group cookings, meetings, suppers, etc. It is also utilized for serving "hot-bar" appetizers for groups of 12 or more following the afternoon hunt. The Cookhouse is avialable year-round for use as a smaller meeting place or for a group cookout.

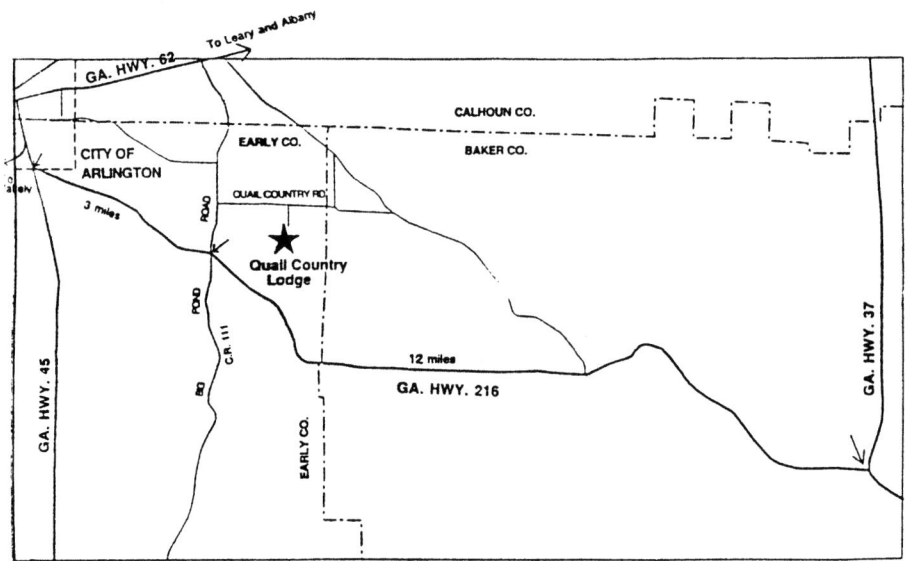

Quail Country

Route 1, Box 745
100 Quail Country Road
Arlington, Georgia 31713

912-725-4645

Website: www.quailcountry.com
E-mail: quail@quailcountry.com

Quail Country Menu

Quail Country
Southern Casserole Breakfast
Mini Blueberry Muffins
Breakfast Casserole
Grits
Fresh Strawberries

Quail Country
Bean Soup Lunch
Pear Salad
Homemade Bean Soup
Corn Sticks
Saltine Crackers
Brownies

Quail Country
Smoked Steak Dinner
Tossed Salad
Smoked Steak
Baked Potato
Yeast Rolls
Pecan Pie

QUAIL COUNTRY

Breakfast Casserole

1   pound mild bulk sausage
4   slices light bread or day-old biscuits, torn into bite-size pieces
12 ounces shredded cheese, divided
8   eggs, lightly beaten
salt and pepper
hot pepper sauce, optional

- Brown sausage and drain well.
- Arrange bread in a single layer in bottom of a greased baking dish. Sprinkle with half of cheese. Top with sausage. Cover with remaining cheese. Pour eggs evenly over cheese. Season with salt and pepper to taste.
- Cover and refrigerate overnight. Uncover and bake in a preheated 350 degree oven for 45 minutes. Serve with hot pepper sauce, if desired. Serves 4.

QUAIL COUNTRY

Homemade Bean Soup

1 cup dried great northern beans
½ pound ham hocks
½ small onion, chopped
salt and pepper
2 cans stewed tomatoes
1 can tomato sauce

- Soak beans, in water to cover, overnight.

- Boil ham hocks and onion in water. Add salt and pepper to taste. When ham hocks have cooked, remove from broth and trim fat. Dice ham and return to broth.

- Add beans and cook at slow boil for 1 hour.

- Add tomatoes and tomato sauce. Continue to simmer until beans are done. Serves 4 to 8.

QUAIL COUNTRY

Quail Country's Smoked Steak

4   (1 to 1¼-inch) thick ribeye steaks, cut fresh
1   cup lemon pepper seasoning
½   cup steak sauce

- Rub both sides of steak with lemon pepper. Lay steaks flat in pan and sprinkle both sides generously with steak sauce. Cover and refrigerate for 3 to 4 hours.

- Smoke steaks over indirect heat, using oak or hickory wood. Cooking time will depend on degree of indirect heat, approximately 1 to 2 hours. These steaks are better served medium.

QUAIL COUNTRY

Corn Sticks

1 cup cornmeal
1 cup all-purpose flour
2 eggs, lightly beaten
¼ cup vegetable oil
1 cup milk
2-4 tablespoons sugar
1 teaspoon baking powder
½ teaspoon salt

- Combine all ingredients and blend thoroughly.

- Pour into a greased cast iron corn stick pan, filling each three-quarters full. Bake in a preheated 425 degree oven until a tester inserted in center comes out clean and sticks are light golden.

Brownies

2 cups sugar
½ cup margarine, softened
4 eggs, lightly beaten
1 cup flour
2 cups chopped pecans
6 tablespoons cocoa
1 teaspoon vanilla

- Combine all ingredients and pour into a greased baking pan.

- Bake in a preheated 350 degree oven until a tester inserted in center comes out clean, about 45 minutes. Serves 6 to 8.

Mama's Pecan Pie

1 cup chopped pecans
1 cup light corn syrup
⅔ cup sugar
pinch of salt
3 eggs, lightly beaten
1 teaspoon vanilla
1 unbaked pie crust

- Combine all ingredients except pie crust. Pour into crust.

- Bake in a preheated 350 degree oven for 1 hour. Serves 8.

Wynfield Plantation

As you wind through beautiful Georgia Pines to Wynfield Plantation, you are surrounded by some of the finest quail habitat in the world—habitat that has made Southwest Georgia famous for its incredible quail hunting. At the end of the driveway to Wynfield, you'll be taken by the rustic beauty of the Main Lodge. As you walk across the wide porch graced with comfortable rocking chairs, a surprise awaits you. Rustic beauty gives way to rustic elegance when you walk through the main entrance into the great room of the Lodge. Here you will enter a world of true Southern comfort as you dine on one of Wynfield's famous savory meals, relax in the Lodge's great room, enjoy coffee or an after dinner drink as you rock on the front porch or retire to the privacy of your own beautiful two-bedroom, fully-equipped cottage.

Wynfield Plantation has a long-standing reputation of excellence as a commercial quail hunting operation and is also well known for its outstanding Southern cuisine and first-class lodging. During the off-season (Quail Season runs from October 1st through March 31st), Wynfield functions as a bed and breakfast inn and also plays host to a great number of corporate and private special events. Along with the excellent fishing available in Woodstock Pond, Wynfield also boasts a world-class sporting clays range, nature trails, and bike paths.

Wynfield was purchased by its current owners in May of 1997, who then constructed the Main Lodge, cottages, sporting clays course, state-of-the-art dog kennels, quail houses, and newly-designed guide headquarters. Wynfield Group Inc., is comprised of owners Dr. Ken Greene, Albany, GA; Ms. Lisa Greene Dasher, Albany, GA; Mr. Joe Hopkins, Folkston, GA; and Dr. Steve Orr, Clinton, S.C. Bill Bowles serves as General Manager of the operation. Wynfield Plantation operated successfully for seven years prior to its sale in 1997, by Larry and Jan Ruis of Albany, GA. The Plantation is named for a relative of the Ruis family and has a long and colorful history dating back to Civil War times. In fact, the original plantation home on the property was used as a hospital during the War Between the States.

Centrally located in the heart of the deep South in Albany, GA, Wynfield Plantation is just a bit more than a one-hour drive from Tallahassee, FL; two hours south of Macon, GA; and a little more than three hours from Atlanta. Each and every experience you have at Wynfield Plantation will leave you with lasting memories of genuine Southern hospitality and some of the finest quail hunting available anywhere!

A warm welcome awaits you at Wynfield Plantation. Your experience with Wynfield is sure to be uniquely Southern and full of generous hospitality and the best hunting available anywhere. For more information or to contact Wynfield, please call (912) 889-0193 or visit their web page at www.wynfieldplantation.com. Their mailing address is Post Office Box 71686, Albany, GA 31708. They look forward to having you as their guest!

Quail Hunting in the Southern Tradition

Quail hunting at Wynfield Plantation is…well, it's just different. It is quail hunting like it is supposed to be! Wynfield offers quail hunting in the Southern tradition where the action is intense, but the atmosphere is relaxed. At Wynfield you will hunt quail on beautiful and challenging courses featuring such terrains as piney woods, wiregrass meadows, fields of broomsage and brush, and lush bottom-lands dotted with hardwoods.

Millie explains the finer points of quail hunting to QU ExecVP Rocky Evans

You will hunt from specially designed jeeps with shooter's platforms and seating to accommodate a party of four plus a non-shooting rider. You can bring your own dogs and house them in Wynfield Plantation's guest kennels or enjoy the convenience of using a brace of their own outstanding dogs. Wynfield's guides know quail hunting like no others. Not only do they know where to find quail, they know what the quail hunting experience is all about…and they know how to help you enjoy it!

Quail hunting is available in full or half day hunts. Guns are available for use and complimentary hunting licenses are provided. Wynfield's pro shop carries all other hunting essentials necessary for your stay.

Combination Hunts

One of the greatest benefits of maintaining the ideal quail hunting habitat is that it will also attract a side variety of other game. Our population of deer, turkey, and wild boar have grown tremendously in recent years creating opportunities for hunters to experience a wide variety of challenging hunts. If you desire to further enhance your visit to Wynfield Plantation, Wynfield offers combination hunts including deer, turkey, and wild boar.

Superb Fishing…At Woodstork Pond

Not only is Southwest Georgia famous for its quail hunting, the fishing is also legendary. At Wynfield you will find superb fishing for bass, bream and catfish. Bring your own boat and tackle or Wynfield will provide everything you need. All you need is your fish skills and some say the fishing is so good you don't even need skill!

World-Class Sporting Clays…

    Need to sharpen your shooting skills before a hunt…keep sharp during the off-season…enjoy an outing with friends…or participate in a shooting competition sanctioned by the National and Georgia chapters of the National Skeet and Clay Shooting Associations? You can experience all of this year-round at Wynfield. Designed by world renowned clay course designer Marty Fischer, Wynfield's course has 21 different shooting boxes spread over 10 acres of natural habitat. Whether it is a pair of targets launched into the pine trees to simulate a rising covey of quail, a target flying above the "gator hole" to simulate incoming ducks, a clay launched from a 50′ tower to simulate an incoming dove, or a target zooming across the ground to mimic a scampering rabbit, Wynfield's course offers a challenge for shooters of every skill level. Join us for a wonderful experience shooting with friends in the natural beauty of the pine forests of Wynfield Plantation.

WYNFIELD PLANTATION

Crispy Buttermilk Fried Corn

¾ cup self-rising flour
¾ cup yellow cornmeal
1¼ cups buttermilk
pepper
2 cups or more corn kernels
(4 large ears)
salt

- Combine flour, cornmeal, buttermilk and pepper to taste. Add enough corn to make batter thick.

- Drop by teaspoonfuls into hot 1-inch-deep oil. Brown of both sides. Drain well and salt to taste.

Hot and Flaky Wynfield Chicken Pie

4 pounds frozen chicken
1 teaspoon salt
pepper
5 carrots, sliced
6 potatoes, peeled and cubed
4 celery stalks, chopped
1 large Vidalia onion, chopped
1 cup butter
1 cup flour
10 cups chicken broth
1 cup half-and-half
1 cup sour cream
¼ cup white cooking wine
2 cans peas, drained
unbaked pie crust or puff pastry

- Place chicken in a large stock pot. Cover with water. Add salt and pepper to taste. Bring to a boil, reduce heat and simmer until chicken is done. Remove chicken from broth to cool. When cool, debone.

- Place carrots and potatoes in a medium saucepan and add enough chicken broth to cover. Bring to a boil, reduce heat, cover and cook until tender.

- Sauté celery and onion in melted butter until tender. Sprinkle in flour and stir until smooth. Stir in 10 cups chicken broth. Add half-and-half, sour cream and wine. Cook, stirring, until thick and bubbly. Add chicken, peas, carrots and potatoes. Salt and pepper to taste.

- Divide chicken mixture among 12 individual pie plates. Top with your favorite pie crust or puff pastry.

- Bake in a preheated 400 degree oven until golden brown, about 30 minutes.

Chocolate Chunk Cookie Dough Cheesepie

Chocolate Crust:

2½ cups crushed chocolate sandwich cookies, with filling
5 tablespoons butter, melted

Filling:

2 (3-ounce) packages cream cheese, softened
⅓ cup sugar
⅓ cup sour cream
1 egg
½ teaspoon vanilla

Cookie Dough:

2 tablespoons butter, softened
¼ cup firmly packed light brown sugar
¼ cup all-purpose flour
1 tablespoon water
¼ teaspoon vanilla
1 cup semisweet chocolate chunks or chips

- For Crust: Preheat oven to 350 degrees. Finely grind cookies, including filling, in food processor. Combine with melted butter and press into bottom and up sides of a pie plate.

- For Filling: Place cream cheese and sugar in a small mixing bowl. Beat on medium speed until smooth. Blend in sour cream, egg and vanilla. Pour into prepared crust.

- For Cookie Dough: Beat butter and brown sugar in a small mixing bowl until light and fluffy. Add flour, water and vanilla and beat until blended. Stir in chocolate.

- Drop cookie dough by teaspoonfuls evenly onto cream cheese mixture. Bake until almost set in center, 35 to 40 minutes. Cool completely on a wire rack. Cover and refrigerate. Serves 8.

Succulent Grilled Quail

This recipe is so easy you will not believe its sophisticated taste and presentation!

- Marinate desired number of quail in one part red wine vinegar to three parts bottled Italian salad dressing. Make sure quail are completely covered by marinade and sealed in a closed container. Marinate for 24 hours in the refrigerator.

- When ready to grill, season quail individually to taste with fresh basil, onion powder, garlic powder and freshly ground black pepper. Wrap each quail in generous slabs of country-cured bacon and grill until desired tenderness.

- Enjoy!

WYNFIELD PLANTATION

WYNFIELD PLANTATION

Spiced Georgia Peach Jam

4 cups chopped ripe Georgia peaches
¼ cup lemon juice
7½ cups sugar
1 teaspoon cinnamon
½ teaspoon ground cloves
½ teaspoon allspice
3 ounces liquid fruit pectin

- Combine peaches and lemon juice in a large saucepan. Add sugar and spices and mix well.

- Place over high heat and bring to a full rolling boil. Boil for 1 minute, stirring constantly.

- Remove from heat and stir in pectin immediately. Skim off foam and cool slightly. Stir, skimming off foam, for 5 minutes.

- Ladle into hot sterilized jars and seal. Makes 3 pints of delicious Georgia peach jam. We serve it with another Wynfield Plantation specialty, our own home-made hot and flaky biscuits and buttery croissants!

WYNFIELD PLANTATION

Plantation Favorites

PLANTATION FAVORITES

Hush Puppies

1 cup white cornmeal
⅓ cup all-purpose flour
1 teaspoon dark brown sugar
   Salt and pepper
⅓ cup milk
2 teaspoons vegetable oil
1 egg

- Combine cornmeal, flour and brown sugar. Season with salt and pepper to taste.
- Mix milk, oil and egg in a separate bowl. Pour into dry mixture. Blend, adding a little water if necessary, but leaving batter thick enough for a spoon to stand in.
- Fill a frying pan 1½ inches deep with oil. Heat over medium high heat. Drop batter by tablespoonfuls into hot oil. Cook until golden brown and floating. Drain well on paper towels.

Roasted Asparagus

2 pounds fresh asparagus
2 tablespoons olive oil
salt and pepper

- Cut ends off asparagus. Brush with olive oil and season with salt and pepper to taste. Place on a baking sheet.
- Roast in a preheated 450 degree oven until lightly browned and tender.

Squash Casserole

1 large onion, chopped
2 tablespoons butter
4 cups cooked squash
1 cup grated carrots
1 can cream of chicken soup
½ cup sour cream
2 cups bread crumbs, divided
salt and pepper

- Preheat oven to 350 degrees.
- Sauté onions in butter until tender. Stir in squash, carrots, soup, sour cream and 1 cup bread crumbs. Season to taste with salt and pepper. Cook 5 minutes, stirring.
- Transfer to a buttered casserole dish. Top with remaining bread crumbs. Bake for 25 to 30 minutes.

PLANTATION FAVORITES

Grilled Barbecue Duck Breast

4 (8-ounce) duck breasts
4 tablespoons soy sauce
1 teaspoon lemon pepper
seasoned salt
½ cup butter, melted

Sauce:
1 cup ketchup
1 cup vinegar
4 tablespoons mustard
juice and minced peel of
 ½ lemon
salt and pepper to taste
½ teaspoon cayenne pepper
1 tablespoon brown sugar
¼ cup butter
2 tablespoons Worcestershire
 sauce

- Rub duck with soy sauce, lemon pepper and seasoned salt to taste. Marinate for 20 minutes.

- Cook on a grill over low heat for 1 to 1½ hours, basting every 20 minutes with butter. Serve with sauce.

- For Sauce: Combine all ingredients in a saucepan. Bring to a boil, reduce heat and simmer.

Grilled Beef and Vegetable Brochettes

1 cup red wine
¼ cup olive oil
1 teaspoon chopped garlic
1 tablespoon rosemary
1 tablespoon thyme
1 teaspoon salt
½ teaspoon pepper
2½ pounds lean, boneless beef, cut in 1½-inch cubes
12 mushrooms
2 green bell peppers, cubed
1 onion, cubed
12 cherry or grape tomatoes
12 wooden skewers, soaked in water

- Combine red wine, olive oil, garlic, rosemary, thyme, salt and pepper in a large bowl. Whisk until well combined.

- Place beef in a bowl and cover with red wine mixture. Toss well to coat. Refrigerate for at least 1 hour.

- Remove beef from marinade and thread on skewers alternately with mushrooms, bell peppers, onion cubes and tomatoes.

- Grill on an oiled rack over medium coals for 8 to 10 minutes, turning occasionally. Serve over rice. Serves 6.

PLANTATION FAVORITES

Blueberry/Peach Pie

Crust:
- 2 cups all-purpose flour
- 1 teaspoon salt
- 2 teaspoons light brown sugar
- ¼ cup pecan meal
- ½ cup unsalted butter, chilled and cut into small pieces
- ¼ cup ice water
- 1 egg white

sugar

Filling:
- 9 medium ripe peaches, peeled, pitted and sliced
- 1 pint blueberries, picked over and rinsed
- 1 cup firmly packed light brown sugar
- ½ cup all-purpose flour

- For Crust: Place flour, salt, brown sugar, pecan meal and butter in a mixing bowl with a paddle attachment. Mix until the dough resembles a coarse, dry meal. Add water at once and mix for 2 to 3 turns. Remove from bowl.

- Work the dough by hand until it forms a mass. Divide in half, shape into 2 disks, cover and refrigerate 30 minutes. Place each disk between sheets of wax paper and roll each into a circle about 12 inches in diameter.

- Place a disk in bottom of a 9-inch pie plate, overlapping 1 inch all around. Brush entire surface with egg white.

- For Filling: Place peaches and blueberries in a bowl. Sprinkle with sugar and let stand 10 minutes. Add flour and mix until it is incorporated.

- Transfer filling to pie plate. Cover with remaining crust. Turn seams under and crimp together. Brush with egg white and sprinkle with sugar.

- Bake in a preheated 375 degree oven for 45 minutes.

PLANTATION FAVORITES

PLANTATION FAVORITES

Country-Style Venison with Gravy

2 pounds (¾-inch-thick) venison tenderloin or (¾-inch) cubes venison ham
salt and pepper
1 cup red wine
2 tablespoons soy sauce
1 teaspoon lemon pepper
flour for dredging
2 medium onions, thinly sliced
⅓ cup flour
3 beef bouillon cubes
1 can cream of mushroom soup
dash of cayenne pepper
1 teaspoon browning sauce

- Place venison in a bowl and salt and pepper lightly. Cover with wine and soy sauce. Season with lemon pepper. Marinate 2 hours.

- Boil onions until tender and drain well.

- Drain venison and dredge in flour. Pour 1½ inches oil in a frying pan and heat. Brown venison on all sides. Sauté onions until dark brown. Drain oil, returning 4 tablespoons to pan.

- Heat to medium-high. Add ⅓ cup flour and stir until dark brown. Slowly stir in enough water to make a smooth, thin mixture. Add bouillon cubes, soup and cayenne. Season with salt and pepper to taste. Add onions and browning sauce.

- Return venison to pan and bring to a simmer. Cook 2 to 3 hours, stirring every half hour to prevent sticking. Add water, if gravy becomes too thick.

Sweet Potatoes Anna

3-4 large sweet potatoes
¾ cup melted butter
¼ cup granulated garlic
1 cup grated Parmesan cheese
salt and pepper

- Peel and thinly slice potatoes. Place a quarter of the potatoes in a baking dish which has been coated with non-stick spray. Pour a quarter of the butter over potatoes. Sprinkle with a quarter of the garlic and top with ½ cup cheese. Season with salt and pepper to taste. Repeat layering 3 times.

- Cover dish with foil and bake in a preheated 400 degree oven for 30 minutes. Remove foil and bake an additional 15 minutes.

PLANTATION FAVORITES

PLANTATION FAVORITES

Country-Style Venison with Gravy

2 pounds (¾-inch-thick) venison tenderloin or (¾-inch) cubes venison ham
salt and pepper
1 cup red wine
2 tablespoons soy sauce
1 teaspoon lemon pepper
flour for dredging
2 medium onions, thinly sliced
⅓ cup flour
3 beef bouillon cubes
1 can cream of mushroom soup
dash of cayenne pepper
1 teaspoon browning sauce

- Place venison in a bowl and salt and pepper lightly. Cover with wine and soy sauce. Season with lemon pepper. Marinate 2 hours.

- Boil onions until tender and drain well.

- Drain venison and dredge in flour. Pour 1½ inches oil in a frying pan and heat. Brown venison on all sides. Sauté onions until dark brown. Drain oil, returning 4 tablespoons to pan.

- Heat to medium-high. Add ⅓ cup flour and stir until dark brown. Slowly stir in enough water to make a smooth, thin mixture. Add bouillon cubes, soup and cayenne. Season with salt and pepper to taste. Add onions and browning sauce.

- Return venison to pan and bring to a simmer. Cook 2 to 3 hours, stirring every half hour to prevent sticking. Add water, if gravy becomes too thick.

Sweet Potatoes Anna

3-4 large sweet potatoes
¾ cup melted butter
¼ cup granulated garlic
1 cup grated Parmesan cheese
salt and pepper

- Peel and thinly slice potatoes. Place a quarter of the potatoes in a baking dish which has been coated with non-stick spray. Pour a quarter of the butter over potatoes. Sprinkle with a quarter of the garlic and top with ½ cup cheese. Season with salt and pepper to taste. Repeat layering 3 times.

- Cover dish with foil and bake in a preheated 400 degree oven for 30 minutes. Remove foil and bake an additional 15 minutes.

INDEX

A
Almond Mandarin Orange Salad 93
Andouille Sausage and Sweet Potato Soup 11
APPLES
   Apple-Cranberry Compote 96
   Baked Apple Pudding with Brandy Sauce 41
ARTICHOKES
   Artichoke and Spinach Casserole 91
ASPARAGUS
   Asparagus Casserole 24
   Hot and Sour Seared Yellowfin Tuna with a
      Bacon Asparagus and New Potato Salad
      and Green Pesto 62
   Roasted Asparagus 120
AVOCADOS
   Chilled Avocado, Tomato and
      Silver Queen Corn Soup 12

B
Baked Quail 28
BBQ Sauce 73
BEANS & PEAS
   Field Pea, Tomato & Buffalo Mozzarella Salad ... 10
   Homemade Bean Soup 106
   Mary Alice's Layered Salad 94
BEEF
   Grilled Beef and Vegetable Brochettes 122
   Quail Country's Smoked Steak 107
BLUEBERRIES
   Blueberry/Peach Pie 124
Braised Venison Steaks 26
Brandy Sauce 41
BREADS
   Bread Pudding 51
   Corn Sticks 108
   Crawfish, Pancetta and Tomato Bruschetta 9
   Grandmother's Gingerbread 75
   Hush Puppies 120
   Mooney's Sour Cream Cornbread 93
BREAKFAST & BRUNCH
   Breakfast Casserole 105
   Pinway Breakfast Casserole 92
   Plantation Cheese Grits 92
BROCCOLI
   Zesty Lemon Sesame Broccoli 40

C
Cabin Bluff Wild Rice 37
CAKES
   Chocolate Chip Cake 52
   Ruth's Sour Cream Pound Cake 97
CARROTS
   Hot and Flaky Wynfield Chicken Pie 113
   Plantation Quail Dinner in a Bag 95
CASSEROLES
   Artichoke and Spinach Casserole 91
   Asparagus Casserole 24
   Breakfast Casserole 105
   Duck and Wild Rice Casserole 96
   Hot Pineapple Casserole 25
   Pinway Breakfast Casserole 92
   Pork Chop Casserole 26
   Potato Casserole 24
   Squash Casserole 120
CHEESE
   Breakfast Casserole 105
   Cappicola Ham, Boursin Cheese
      and Leek Crêpe 63
   Field Pea, Tomato & Buffalo Mozzarella Salad ... 10
   Glorious Macaroni 24
   Grilled Quail with Smoked Gouda Grits
      and Tomato Gravy 15
   Mary Alice's Layered Salad 94
   Pinway Breakfast Casserole 92
   Plantation Cheese Grits 92
   Roast Rack of Lamb with Blue Corn Chip
      and Basil Crust, Mongolian Fire Pot Sausage,
      Couscous and a Smoked Cheddar and
      Horseradish Sauce 60
   Southern Pimiento Cheese 91
CHICKEN
   Chicken Breast in Wine and Mushroom Sauce 81
   Chicken Pot Pie 50
   Hot and Flaky Wynfield Chicken Pie 113
   Southern Fried Chicken 48
   Stuffed and Wrapped Chicken Breasts 84
CHOCOLATE
   Brownies 108
   Chocolate Chip Cake 52
   Chocolate Chunk Cookie Dough Cheesepie ... 114
COOKIES
   Chocolate Chunk Cookie Dough Cheesepie ... 114
   Lemon Sugar Cookies 41
CORN
   Chilled Avocado, Tomato and
      Silver Queen Corn Soup 12
   Corn Sticks 108
   Crispy Buttermilk Fried Corn 113
Crab Cakes with Dill Sauce 38
CRANBERRIES
   Apple-Cranberry Compote 96
CREPES
   Cappicola Ham, Boursin Cheese
      and Leek Crêpe 63

D
DESSERTS
   Amaretto Brownies 97
   Apple-Cranberry Compote 96
   Brownie Honey and Maple Syrup Cheesecake
      with Peanut Brittle Sauce 66
   Brownies 108
   Dad's Fruit Cobbler 75
   Park Avenue Squares 98
   Peach Cobbler 51
   Warm Fried Green Tomato Tart with
      Chinese Five Spice Ice Cream 64
Dill Sauce 38
DOVE
   Baked Dove Breasts 50
   Dove Delicious 94
DUCK
   Duck and Wild Rice Casserole 96
   Grilled Barbecue Duck Breast 121

F
FISH
   Broiled Speckled Trout 39
   Crawfish, Pancetta and Tomato Bruschetta 9
   Hot and Sour Seared Yellowfin Tuna with a
      Bacon Asparagus and New Potato Salad
      and Green Pesto 62
   Salmon Patties 50
FRUIT
   Dad's Fruit Cobbler 75
   Spiced Georgia Peach Jam 116

G
GAME
   Baked Dove Breasts 50
   Baked Quail 28
   Braised Venison Steaks 26
   Country-Style Venison with Gravy 126
   Dove Delicious 94
   Duck and Wild Rice Casserole 96
   Fried Quail 82
   Grilled Barbecue Duck Breast 121
   Grilled Quail with Smoked Gouda Grits
      and Tomato Gravy 15
   Pinway Plantation Fried Quail 95
   Plantation Quail Dinner in a Bag 95
   Smothered Quail 37
   Stewed Rabbit and Shiitake Mushrooms
      on Crispy Yukon Potato Hash Cakes 16
   Succulent Grilled Quail 114
Glorious Macaroni 24
Gulf Oysters and Tasso Ham over
   Fried Green Tomatoes 13

H
Hot Pineapple Casserole 25

I
Incredible Crab Soup 25

J
JAMS & JELLIES
   Spiced Georgia Peach Jam 116

L
LAMB
   Roast Rack of Lamb with Blue Corn Chip and
      Basil Crust, Mongolian Fire Pot Sausage,
      Couscous and a Smoked Cheddar and
      Horseradish Sauce 60
LEMONS
   Lemon Sugar Cookies 41

M
Mama's Pecan Pie 108
Mary Alice's Layered Salad 94
Mooney's Sour Cream Cornbread 93
MUSHROOMS
   Chicken Breast in Wine and Mushroom Sauce 81
   Glorious Macaroni 24

Grilled Beef and Vegetable Brochettes 122
Smothered Quail 37
Stewed Rabbit and Shiitake Mushrooms on
   Crispy Yukon Potato Hash Cakes 16

N

NUTS
Almond Mandarin Orange Salad 93
Brownies 108
Mama's Pecan Pie 108
Park Avenue Squares 98
Sesame and Peanut-Crusted Soft Shell Crab on
   Spinach Chiffonade with Creole Horseradish
   Cream and Tamarind-Orange Infusion 14
Southern Pecan Pie 52, 98
Zesty Lemon Sesame Broccoli 40

O

ORANGES
Almond Mandarin Orange Salad 93

P

Park Avenue Squares 98
PASTA
Glorious Macaroni 24
PEACHES
Blueberry/Peach Pie 124
Peach Cobbler 51
Spiced Georgia Peach Jam 116
Peanut Brittle Sauce 66
Pesto 62
PIES
Blueberry/Peach Pie 124
Mama's Pecan Pie 108
Southern Pecan Pie 52, 98
PINEAPPLE
Hot Pineapple Casserole 25
Pinway Breakfast Casserole 92
Plantation Cheese Grits 92
PORK
  Bacon
    Cabin Bluff Wild Rice 37
    Crawfish, Pancetta and Tomato Bruschetta 9
    Dove Delicious 94
    Field Pea, Tomato & Buffalo
      Mozzarella Salad 10
    Grilled Quail with Smoked Gouda
      Grits and Tomato Gravy 15
    Hot and Sour Seared Yellowfin Tuna with a
      Bacon Asparagus and New Potato Salad
      and Green Pesto 62
  Ham
    Cappicola Ham, Boursin Cheese and
      Leek Crêpe 63
    Gulf Oysters and Tasso Ham over
      Fried Green Tomatoes 13
    Homemade Bean Soup 106
    Stuffed and Wrapped Chicken Breasts 84
  Old Fashioned Pig Roast with BBQ Sauce 73
  Pork Chop Casserole 26
  Sausage
    Andouille Sausage and Sweet Potato Soup 11
    Breakfast Casserole 105
    Pinway Breakfast Casserole 92

Roast Rack of Lamb with Blue Corn Chip and
   Basil Crust, Mongolian Fire Pot Sausage,
   Couscous and a Smoked Cheddar and
   Horseradish Sauce 60
POTATOES
Andouille Sausage and Sweet Potato Soup 11
Hot and Flaky Wynfield Chicken Pie 113
Hot and Sour Seared Yellowfin Tuna with a
   Bacon Asparagus and New Potato Salad
   and Green Pesto 62
Potato Casserole 24
Stewed Rabbit and Shiitake Mushrooms on
   Crispy Yukon Potato Hash Cakes 16
Sweet Potatoes Anna 126
PUDDINGS
Baked Apple Pudding with Brandy Sauce 41
Bread Pudding 51

Q

QUAIL
Baked Quail 28
Fried Quail 82
Grilled Quail with Smoked Gouda Grits and Tomato
   Gravy 15
Pinway Plantation Fried Quail 95
Plantation Quail Dinner in a Bag 95
Smothered Quail 37
Succulent Grilled Quail 114
Quail Country's Smoked Steak 107

R

RABBIT
Stewed Rabbit and Shiitake Mushrooms on
   Crispy Yukon Potato Hash Cakes 16
RICE & GRAINS
Baked Dove Breasts 50
Cabin Bluff Wild Rice 37
Duck and Wild Rice Casserole 96
Roast Rack of Lamb with Blue Corn Chip and
   Basil Crust, Mongolian Fire Pot Sausage,
   Couscous and a Smoked Cheddar and
   Horseradish Sauce 60
Shrimp Victoria 28
Roasted Asparagus 120
Ruth's Sour Cream Pound Cake 97

S

SALADS
Almond Mandarin Orange Salad 93
Field Pea, Tomato & Buffalo Mozzarella Salad ... 10
Mary Alice's Layered Salad 94
Mixed Salad with Ginger Vinaigrette 40
Salmon Patties 50
SAUCES
BBQ Sauce 73
Brandy Sauce 41
Dill Sauce 38
Peanut Brittle Sauce 66
Pesto 62
SEAFOOD
  Crab
    Crab Cakes with Dill Sauce 38
    Incredible Crab Soup 25

Sesame and Peanut-Crusted Soft Shell Crab on
   Spinach Chiffonade with Creole Horseradish
   Cream and Tamarind-Orange Infusion 14
Crawfish, Pancetta and Tomato Bruschetta 9
  Oysters
    Gulf Oysters and Tasso Ham over Fried Green
      Tomatoes 13
  Shrimp
    Mom's Shrimp Creole 74
    Shrimp Creole 39
    Shrimp Victoria 28
SOUPS
Andouille Sausage and Sweet Potato Soup 11
Chilled Avocado, Tomato and
   Silver Queen Corn Soup 12
Homemade Bean Soup 106
Incredible Crab Soup 25
Southern Fried Chicken 48
Southern Pimiento Cheese 91
SPINACH
Artichoke and Spinach Casserole 91
Sesame and Peanut-Crusted Soft Shell Crab on
   Spinach Chiffonade with Creole Horseradish
   Cream and Tamarind-Orange Infusion 14
SQUASH
Squash Casserole 120
Stuffed and Wrapped Chicken Breasts 84

T

TOMATOES
Chilled Avocado, Tomato and
   Silver Queen Corn Soup 12
Crawfish, Pancetta and Tomato Bruschetta 9
Field Pea, Tomato & Buffalo Mozzarella Salad ... 10
Grilled Beef and Vegetable Brochettes 122
Grilled Quail with Smoked Gouda Grits
   and Tomato Gravy 15
Gulf Oysters and Tasso Ham over
   Fried Green Tomatoes 13
Homemade Bean Soup 106
Mom's Shrimp Creole 74
Shrimp Creole 39
Warm Fried Green Tomato Tart with
   Chinese Five Spice Ice Cream 64

V

VEGETABLES
Grilled Beef and Vegetable Brochettes 122
VENISON
Braised Venison Steaks 26
Country-Style Venison with Gravy 126

W

Warm Fried Green Tomato Tart with Chinese Five
   Spice Ice Cream 64

Z

Zesty Lemon Sesame Broccoli 40